# Where is the Music?

### the multiple near-death experiences of a world traveler

## Gloria M. Gieseke, M.A.

Password Publications
San Antonio, Texas

Published by Password Publications
8611 Cape Valley
San Antonio, TX 78227-2313

First edition 1999

Artwork: Musician Angel with Lute by Melozzo da Forli (1438-1494) Pinacoteca, Vatican Museum

**Publisher's cataloging-in-Publication**
*(Provided by Quality Books, Inc.)*

Gieseke, Gloria M.
      Where is the music? : the multiple near-death experiences of a world traveler / by Gloria M. Gieseke. -- 1st. ed.
      p.cm.
      ISBN: 0-9672786-0-0

      1. Near-death experiences. 2. Angels. 3. Dreams. 4. Spiritual healing. 5. Gieseke, Gloria M. --Journeys. I. Title.

BF1045.N4G54 1999                    133.9'01'3
                              QB199-843

*To my husband, Cliff,*
*an angel of a man.*

# CONTENTS

# Introduction
## By Dr. Anne Kunath[1]

*Author of "The Art of Making Things Happen"*
*and "What Are you Giving Life To?"*

Over the many years that I have known Gloria Gieseke, I have been aware of her deep spiritual nature. She has a great hunger, not only to practice the presence of God but also to help others in their realization of the presence of God.

Gloria's experiences in her world travels provide an interesting background for the many spiritual experiences through-out her story. For those of us enthralled by her book, it provides history lessons of the many countries she visited and lived in as well as revealing a spellbinding path of enlightenment.

Mrs. Gieseke's near-death experiences explain so well the loving nature of God who is always available to us. It removes the fear of death by offering new insights to the spiritual protection of a loving Father/Mother God.

One of the more interesting insights for me is Gloria's unique ability to bring all religions into focus by honoring each one of them. She combines a joyful attitude of gratitude with the love of all religions. This puts us on a deep level of understanding about the similarity of all religions when we move beyond the dogma, the rules and regulations, and simply return to the love of God expressing through all people everywhere.

Gloria Gieseke has opened a door to new awareness of spiritual insights through her expertise in making the unusual so very acceptable to a questioning world. I suggest that as you begin to read this book you meditate for a few minutes first. Your soul will identify with the beautiful experiences that Gloria describes and will move you into a new level of spiritual growth.

---

[1] *Pastor of the Church of Today, San Antonio, Texas*

## Chapter I

# Where is the Music?
# First Near-Death Experience

Another frightful asthma attack in the middle of the night. It was Tuesday March 2, 1982 and we were living in Riyadh, Saudi Arabia, where, nine months earlier, my husband Cliff had been assigned by the Defense Language Institute to the U.S. Military Training Mission in Riyadh to teach English to the Saudi Arabian land forces.

Badly short of breath, I reached for the inhaler under my pillow, used it once and waited for it to work. Feeling no relief I used it a second time, but my breathing, instead of improving, got even more difficult. My husband, sleeping by my side, woke up noticing my distress and helped me to a chair. Our two boys (ages 13 and 8 at the time), also came into our room to see if they could be of help. The older boy tried to fan my face with a magazine, while my husband got dressed.

Things got worse by the minute and my struggle for breath quickly came to an end when my eyes rolled back and I lapsed into unconsciousness. One of the boys rushed to call for help at one of our neighbors on the same third floor, Navy Lt. Commander Walker, who rapidly got dressed and came to help my husband take me to the Saudi Military Hospital, not far from the U.S. Military Mission compound where we lived.

In the same chair in which I was sitting, they moved me to the elevator and then down to the ground floor to Lt.

Comdr. Walker's car. He drove while my husband held me, blue and unconscious, in the back seat.

Once at the hospital, I was rushed to the emergency room, where the emergency team immediately drew the curtains around a portion of the room and set to revive me.

At another level, at some time during this unconscious period, I fully realized I was dying, and I said to myself: "There is nothing left.... there is no family now.... this is between God and me." I was surrounded by a soft yellow light as far as the horizon. Sweetness, love and peace came to me from this Light and I, in turn, started singing and humming softly to God, to the Light. This loving exchange went on for some time until, at one point, I said: "But beloved God, if I am dying, where is the music?, because I expect to go with music."

In an instant, in a flash, with a jolt I came back to my achy body, ready to engage again in the fight for life. With this, the doctors, too, caught sign of a heartbeat and called to me to answer in some way if I could hear them, by moving a hand or a toe or something. I moved my hand, which somebody was holding.

Under a respirator, IV treatments and periodic shots of Terbutaline a few hours went by in the emergency room, before I was transferred to the Intensive Care Unit, where I spent the next twenty-four hours. After that I was put in a very comfortable private room.

The Egyptian doctor who had worked on me in the emergency room, together with a young Australian doctor, came later to the ICU to listen to my chest and to set up a follow-up treatment. "You are a lucky lady," was his greeting to me.

My feelings were of gratitude towards God, the doctors and the people who had helped save my life. There was also a deep joy and love for life, and a sense of optimism in my words that amazed the persons who had seen me so close to death only hours before, and they expressed this to me the days that followed. After the love and bliss I had so briefly experienced, all these emotions came very naturally and effortlessly to me.

The doctors and the Filipino nurses who took care of me at the Saudi Army Hospital were most caring and loving. I must have had about half a dozen nurses assigned to my care every day. They pampered me in every way, even giving me a manicure and bringing their make-up and beautifying me like their favorite doll. With two of those nurses I talked about my near-death experience and they were both very moved by it. One of them opened her heart to me and confided her deepest religious feelings. She also brought some spiritual poetry for me to read.

My husband Cliff was the first person to hear about my NDE. He is a spiritual man and understood my experience well and, as always, was loving and supportive. He, too, was very grateful to God for sparing my life, without me suffering any brain damage, which was a remarkable thing in itself.

Nine days after I entered the hospital, I was discharged, and by Friday morning I felt well enough to go to mass[2]. Although I was not a practicing Catholic and had been away from the Church for more than twenty years (since the late 50s), going to mass that Friday was for me a heartfelt act of thanksgiving. After arriving in Saudi Arabia in 1981 my husband, a non-Catholic, had become slightly

---

[2] *Mass was held on Friday. Friday is the day of worship in Muslim countries, equivalent to the Christian Sunday.*

interested in the works of the Catholic Church, and we had attended mass a few times at the military compound where we lived. After mass, I impulsively told the priest, Father Eugene, about my NDE. He commented with amazement on the ease with which I had surrendered to God in the face of death, and confessed to me that for him the thought of dying was the most frightening thing in the world.

In Saudi Arabia, going to mass or any other Christian service was a secretive event, because Islam is officially the only religion allowed in the kingdom. Islam is practiced in Saudi Arabia in a very strict way, as the Saudis consider themselves the guardians of the Islamic faith. Nevertheless, the foreign community in the 70s and 80s was larger than the number of nationals, and tending to their spiritual needs was a necessity well acknowledged at the highest level of the Saudi government. So, some of the foreign communities in cities like Riyadh, Jeddah, Dhahran and a few others were allowed to worship very discreetly and unofficially in the privacy of their company's compound. At least that was the attitude of the Saudi government towards Christians. I don't know how others, such as the Buddhists, for example, were allowed to practice their religion. There were hundreds of thousands of non-Christian Japanese, Koreans, Taiwanese, etc. employed or doing business in Saudi Arabia in the 80s when I lived there.

# CHAPTER 2

# The Gift of Dreaming

I have always been a dreamer and a spiritual person, but after my first near-death experience there was a period of accelerated learning and growth, lasting more than a year. I knew I was learning important spiritual truths. Some of the "teachings" would come while asleep, in a way not quite like dreams. Many dreams of a spiritual character also came during that period, to complement and reaffirm the teachings I was receiving. A capacity for analyzing my dreams within the dreaming state became evident at that time, too. The three dreams in this chapter are examples of that gift that I still receive with some frequency. The first one, more than any other, I would love to keep in my heart for all eternity. It happened in September 1982, eight months after the NDE

### *My True Identity*

*In the dream, I came to the entrance of the U.S. Military Training Mission compound where we lived, and the guard at the guardhouse asked me for my ID, as was customary. I opened my purse to look for the card but I stopped when I noticed sparks coming from my heart. I looked carefully and saw, on the upper part of my body, the face and the chest of Jesus Christ overtaking me. His face became my face and his heart my heart, pulsating with light. I stopped right there and told the guard: "This is my true identity; this is who I really am."* End of the dream.

When I woke up, passages of the New Testament came to my mind. Those that mention that "we must put on the Christ," "God within" and "the Christ in us," were the first associations I made. The message, the command, the meaning of the dream, was very clear to me.

In real life, as in my dream, I did live at a U.S. military complex in Riyadh, and everyone entering the compound was required to show a valid ID to the guards at the gate. More than fifty families and many single personnel (military and civilian,) associated with the U.S. Military Mission, lived there in two four-story buildings and several villas. A post office (APO) was also located at the compound, to serve all U.S. government personnel in the area. The Mission also offered the residents of the compound a small library, a swimming pool, a recreation center and a fine restaurant.

### The Bread is Rising

*In the dream, three women I knew (they lived at the Mission,) came to my door, each one with a Bible under her arm and said to me: "Gloria, we are here to teach you how to make bread."*

*"But ladies," I answered, "I already know how to make bread. I have known for a long time. In fact, my bread is already rising. Come and see."*

*I took them to another room where in a deep shiny stainless steel, or silver container (big and tall like a barrel), the whitest bread was coming out of the edges.* End of the dream.

This dream came at a time when I felt dissatisfied with the atmosphere and narrow-mindedness of a Bible class I had joined at the compound. The three ladies in my dream, plus about six or seven more, were part of our weekly Bible class. Most of them were either Catholic, Protestant or born-again Christians. For some members of the group, meditators, lovers or respecters of all religions and yoga students (and I was all of that,) were suspected of being in mortal sin, blasphemous and even satanic. One of the women in my dream had actually said to me on one occasion: "Meditation is a thing of the devil." She had also reacted angrily when one of the women in the group had invited a Filipino man, who worked at the recreation center where we met weekly, to stay for the class. She exploded: "No, he can't stay! His god is not our god!! That to me was blasphemy. I answered, feeling really ashamed: "The same old God who created you, created him; he is a child of God; the "God of all creation." The man, a Muslim who had been a boxer in his youth, left the room.

Here was a woman with considerable education, the wife of a lieutenant colonel, who professed to be a Catholic and a 'born again Christian,' showing less than Christian qualities. Most of my classmates were married to U.S. military officers; one was married to an Air Force master sergeant, and myself, married to a civilian.

Other than studying some chapters of the Bible, to the letter, the women directed their efforts to defending their beliefs from heathen contamination, and to showing me that I was going on a "clear and sure path to hell." The idea of getting close to any other religion was horrifying to them. They even advised each other not to go to any doctor who was not a Christian. There were thousands of foreign doctors working in hospitals all over Saudi Arabia, and probably hundreds of them in the capital itself, but who would want to go around asking them about their religion. I told those ladies I would accept help and goodness from whomever and wherever I could find it. And I did. During my two years in Riyadh I saw a Pakistani, a Syrian, an Egyptian and an Australian doctor. I bet most of them were not Christian, but they all showed compassion and diligence in treating me every time imminent asthma trouble brought me to their offices.

The idea of reincarnation was a scary thing to these women. As far as they were concerned, this life was all there was; a one-shot event, and nothing else to follow but heaven or hell. "God is a jealous god," they would read from the Book, to warn me about my "wrong thinking," telling me they were praying for my salvation. I would usually answer them: "Thank you, prayers are never wasted." And that is true.

It was becoming clear to me that they were on a mission to change me, and I probably was on one too, although not that drastic. I was not peddling any religion in particular, and I didn't want the class to turn into a verbal 'holy war,' either. What I hoped was for them to show some understanding, tolerance and a healthy curiosity for other people's religions. So, when that dream about the 'rising bread' came to me, I knew it was a sign for me to quit the group. I thanked them, wished them success with their studies and said good bye to the class.

To pass the time, I applied, and got a job at the Mission's library, three days a week. Another lady from outside the compound, worked the remaining three days. I liked the job well and learned the routine quickly. No special qualifications were required, except courtesy and care. The patrons, adults and children, seem pleased with us, and our small library was a busy place.

Fanatics, however, don't know when to stop. When the librarian I was working with had to return to the U.S., my old Bible study classmate, married to an Air Force master sergeant, intrigued a bit and got the soon-to-be-vacant job. Not long after she started working, fewer and fewer people visited the library during her shift (daily attendance was recorded), and some patrons complained to me about the rudeness and hot temper of the new lady. Then I started noticing that, after my day off, sometimes I would come to work and find books missing from specific categories on the shelves, and find no record of them being on loan to the patrons. This was a serious matter, and when I asked H. about the missing books, she told me she had put them away in boxes, because she felt they contained "occult and un-Christian materials."

We had no more than two dozen books on philosophy, world religions, self-help, psychology, etc. and almost half of them she had labeled "occultism." Her "raids," however, were directed especially at the science-fiction shelves. She was determined to keep certain books away from the readers. On top of that, she wanted a say in deciding what books to order from the U.S. government agency in charge of supplying a small number of books every month (on loan only, for up to 90 days) to libraries for the U.S. armed forces overseas, like ours. Ordering those books was supposed to be based on requests from the patrons, without the librarian's personal taste having anything to do with the choices.

When I informed our employer about the situation, he was reluctant to take any action, because the woman had been "recommended" by some high official in the

Mission. I decided to quit, inform some high-ranking patrons, and let H. swim or sink. Two weeks later she was fired and two people from outside the Mission were hired to replace us.

### Grace onto grace

*In this dream I found myself overlooking a vast field of white flowers. As I crossed the length of the field leaping joyfully in the air, I noticed the flowers were Easter lilies, and they were opening up, row after row, as I passed over them.* End of the dream.

I knew at the time, this was another spiritual dream, and I cherished it, but the title "grace onto grace" came two years later, in 1983, when back in the States, I told this dream to the minister of the non-denominational church my family and I had attended before going to Saudi Arabia. The minister, a very spiritual lady I had known for a few years, had just those three short and fitting words to say about the dream.

As I was going over the above paragraph, months after I had written this chapter, I became aware of one tangible meaning of the field of flowers opening up for me: I had turned into a gardener, of all places in a desert city of Saudi Arabia (Riyadh, where so little in the way of green-ery or flowers was seen), after my first near-death experi-ence. For years I was convinced that every flower I plant-ed would just die, because that is how many earlier attempts had ended up. But gardening was a different story after 1982. It started in our apartment with some cuttings a neighbor gave me and, to my surprise, in two weeks or so the small pot was full of colorful, healthy red coleus. Soon, cuttings from those cuttings gave me enough for another planter to adorn the large living room of our apartment. When my family and I went on a two-week vacation to Spain in May 1982, I bought several packets of seeds to try to grow more exotic varieties of coleus. I became so successful at it that my luscious plants became a money-making hobby for the rest of our stay in Saudi Arabia.

My "green thumb" is still helping flowers bloom all around my house in San Antonio, Texas. Once a year I have to have a garage sale (mostly a plant sale) when I run out of shelves and space inside and outside to put my flower and herb pots. My double impatients, for example, have been so prolific that a few dozen planters, plastic milk jugs and big yogurt tubs are still lining the back and front of my house, full of blooms in the pleasant cool days of winter 1998 in south Texas. Plants can give such joy to your soul.

# CHAPTER 3

# Shop, Shop, Shop

As I said earlier, in the mid 1980s the number of foreigners working in Saudi Arabia outnumbered the nationals two to one. Oil was king and the country's modernization had been going full steam for more than a decade; the kingdom could afford the best of help in every field. Skyscrapers, highways and residential construction was going on at a feverish pace in the capital and all major cities. One of the biggest airports in the world was also being constructed at that time in Riyadh to accommodate the millions of pilgrims arriving once a year for the Haj[3]. In the 1980s you could also find some of the most modern, luxurious and best-staffed and equipped hospitals in the world in Saudi Arabia's main cities. Large numbers of foreign women came to the kingdom lured by the relatively good wages they could earn working as nurses and even as maids; the largest group was made up of mostly single women from Asian countries. By comparison, the number of western women working in Saudi Arabia was relatively small.

For the wives of foreigners working in Saudi Arabia there was very little to do in the capital, except for shopping. We could not drive or even walk alone on the streets of Riyadh. The dress code was very strict for all women, and social life was restricted to the privacy of your own compound. There was no public entertainment such as

---

[3] *The pilgrimage to the holy city of Mecca that Muslims are required to make at least once in their life.*

movie theaters, swimming pools, etc.; nor were there public libraries or museums where you could explore and spend some time. The one government-operated television channel was dedicated almost exclusively to religious matters. The restrictions were especially hard on single people, having few opportunities to get together with other singles. To compensate for this many foreign companies and Saudi employers gave their single employees an out-of-country vacation every six months.

Western women were advised to wear long dresses with long sleeves and high necks; no tight blouses, sweaters or pants were allowed. A few women, though, dared to wear jeans occasionally outside their compound but were promptly persuaded by the religious police to change their minds. The religious police, made up of old men carrying a cane or a switch, walked the streets and would come behind any woman wearing inappropriate attire and whip her legs and then take her to a police station for a reprimand. If the woman was married, her husband was called immediately to respond for his wife's offense and to promise and sign a document assuming responsibility for her modesty. Repeat offenders would be expelled from the country. I witnessed those old men whipping women's legs several times while shopping in downtown Riyadh. For a while, in 1982, foreign women were required to wear a full black cape over their shoulders, called the "abayah." It was the same kind of cover Saudi women wore in the street besides the veil over their faces. The garment was rather cumbersome and hot in the typical outdoor temperatures of 100-115 degrees or more and it caused many complains on the part of the foreigners. After less than a year the requirement of the abayah was lifted; the Saudis concluded that the foreign women had not worn the abayah with the dignity it required.

The zuq or bazaar in downtown Riyadh was a fun place to shop and partly made up for the amenities and mobility we were missing. Our compound provided us with two minibuses for weekly shopping trips. Anything from spices, to shoes, to carpets could be purchased in the hundreds of shops clustered in one big market. The gold zuq was the most impressive thing you could ever see. Gold in all forms and shapes was displayed in cases and also covered the walls of the shops (dozens of shops) from floor to ceiling. I dare to say that not a single woman, foreign or local was not fond of and a regular visitor to the gold zuq; with nothing better to do, women filled the zuqs daily. The precious metal, all of it 18K or purer, was sold by weight regardless of the artistry of the piece, according to the price set daily by the world gold market. Bars from the Swiss Bank, in a variety of weights was the preferred investment among the foreigners, with chunky necklaces and bracelets a close second choice.

Vendors, shopkeepers, office clerks and anybody taking care of customers were always males. There were companies that employed women, but they (foreign women, too) were kept apart from men and out of sight. I learned that traditionally in Saudi Arabia the man does the grocery shopping for the family or women relatives, since a woman's place in the Islamic tradition is the home. That explains why it was so rare to see veiled women in the isles of the supermarkets. But at the zuqs they rubbed elbows with us all the time and felt very much at ease with us foreigners, and us with them, even exchanging greetings and simple phrases in English sometimes. One older Saudi woman I met at the zuq one day told me she had lived in England with her grandchildren and had learned some English there. As we said goodbye, she, unexpectedly, gave me a big hug, and I hugged her back. You find that kind of spontaneity from loving souls in every corner of the world, I am happy to say, and it can really make your day.

But not all showings of affection were so innocent and welcomed. Many foreign women found themselves the object of unwanted remarks and fondling from shopkeepers and vendors who somehow had the idea that foreign women were easy or not entitled to the same respect due their veiled Moslem counterparts. Some friends of mine had been touched more than once while shopping, usually on their breast while they were alone or when there were few people around in the shop. I had a cashier hold and caress my hand in his hands, in a store once, as I extended my hand to receive the change due to me. It was so disconcerting for me to see this young man's serene expression as I retrieved my hand in surprise, that my reaction was more one of wonder and pity than an angry one. I left the store thinking Moslem men probably didn't get enough loving from their mothers or wives. This wouldn't be strange at all, given the strict separation of the sexes and the few opportunities for friendship and interaction between young men and women in Saudi Arabia, the most conservative of all the Islamic countries in the world. Of course, these episodes were annoying and embarrassing, but they were far less malicious than the grabbing and harassment foreign women were subjected to in Iran in the 1960s and 1970s, under the Shah, when foreigners flooded the country lured by Iran's economic boom.

Other than those kinds of irritations, Saudi Arabia was a peaceful and safe place in which to live and work. Violent crime was almost unheard of and theft and petty crime were also uncommon. Justice was carried out swiftly under Islamic law. Punishment ranging from the loss of a limb for theft to decapitation for murder was enough, it appeared, to deter most would be criminals in that society. Foreigners learned not to go shopping downtown on Fridays or they might be forced to stand on the front row and witness the public executions carried out in Riyadh in front of the Ministry of Justice, not far from the zuq (market.) Even on Saturdays the blood might still be there as a grisly reminder to passers-by. On one occasion I and several women from my compound saw a bloody white robe resting on the executioners block, as we passed by on the way to one of the entrances to the zuq; not a sight I want to see again.

My family and I learned a few more things about the Islamic society we were living in, from direct contact with Saudis or from people who knew its customs well. Part of that knowledge came from a woman I became very fond of, who had lived in Saudi Arabia thirty-four years when I met her. She had been born in Colombia to a Colombian mother and a Palestinian immigrant. At age twelve she and her family had gone to Palestine (a section Israel took later), and at age fifteen was given in marriage to a man she had never met, following a traditional middle eastern custom. The marriage had worked out well for forty years already when I met her and her family. Three of her six living children were still at home and attending college in 1982 when I first met them. She had lost three children to malnutrition and disease during their first years in Saudi

Arabia, when medical attention was a far cry from the modern facilities of the 1980s I had used, and the food supply very limited and much of it out of reach of the average family. Eating a tomato or a salad in those days, she told me, was a treat reserved for those close to the royal family. Once in a while, on holidays, her husband would receive a gift of fruit or vegetables from his very rich bosses, which to my friend was a gift more valuable than gold. Riyadh in the late 1940s was just a small desert town with more camels than people. In that barren and harsh environment, many children died in early childhood.

My friend's youngest daughter was in her early twenties a student at one of Riyadh's women's universities. She was also a member of her alma mater's belly dancing group. We saw her dance at her home to live music played by her father and brother on lutes, and she was quite an artist; much better belly dancing than anything you'll see in the West. The young woman was engaged to be married to a young Saudi, and, to show me how serious the marriage plans were, her mother told me her future son-in-law had already seen her daughter in a swimming suit, by the pool side. That was a measure of how far their courtship had gone, and by Saudi standards it had gone plenty far. I laughed inside myself thinking how irrelevant a situation like that would be in the western world where kissing among young people or even sleeping together doesn't have to imply any commitment for the future.

I was made aware of an even stranger custom by another friend (from Ecuador) married to a Saudi Arabian. It was that baby girls can be promised in marriage to another family soon after they are born. Her own little girl (two years old at the time) had received three offers and expensive gifts from three different families before she was one year old, my friend told me with pride. The custom applied only to baby girls. She also had two small sons.

On the subject of how many wives a Muslim is entitled to have, my husband heard from some of his students that four wives is the maximum number allowed, if the man can afford to do so and treats them equally well. In modern times, however, few men take advantage of that option. The students said it was not that uncommon for older men to have two wives, but the younger generations were opting for marrying just one woman. In checking this information against the holy Qur'an (the Koran), I found in Surah IV, verse 3 the same counsel.

In Riyadh I had the opportunity to visit with the family of one of my husband's students. My husband and I arrived at his home and were greeted by three men, one of them the Saudi officer who had invited us. We took off our shoes and shook hands with them in the living room. Then one of the men showed me to another room. I found four unveiled women waiting for me in yet another living room. One young woman spoke rather good English and translated the whole conversation. We talked about family, travel, food, customs in Saudi Arabia, the United States, my country, etc., and had coffee and pastries. I learned that there is always a veil or two ready to use, behind the main door, in case one of the women in the house has to answer the door. The males in the immediate family as well as cousins and uncles can look at an unveiled female relative, but no other man, Saudi or foreigner can see a woman's face without the veil. When asked if they liked to be behind the veil in public, they were unanimous in saying it helps to keep them safe and respected.

Another occasion to mingle socially with Saudi women came at a wedding we were invited to. This time the sister of a Saudi officer, second in command at the school where my husband taught English, was getting married. Another American teacher, Roger, and his wife Robin were invited too. When we arrived the wedding had already taken place and the party had started. Lots of men, in their finest white tunics and headdress, were sitting on carpets in circles, chatting or listening to the live music playing outside the large two-story house were the celebration was being held. Roger, my husband and our two children joined the men's group, while Robin and I were led to the second floor where the female friends and relatives of the bride were having a separate celebration. Meanwhile the bride, as tradition dictates, was kept locked in one of the rooms, unavailable to anybody except the bridegroom, who could enter her room anytime through a side door. An older matron sat guarding the front door, so that the bride would not be disturbed. Later, at the insistence of one of the hostesses, we were allowed to step into that room and greet the bride. We understood this was bending the tradition a little bit and a privilege for Robin and me.

The women guests (more than a hundred) kept themselves entertained dancing with each other to the beat of a live orchestra (made up of women, of course), or sitting on carpets drinking Arab coffee, chatting and laughing. Coffee was being served every few minutes. The particular kind of coffee they were serving is hard for most westerners to get used to. It is made with almost green, ground coffee beans and cardamom, and then strained through some woven twigs in the shape of a bird's nest, which gives the brew a very bitter and, for me, unpalatable taste. It is served in tiny cups, maybe smaller than a demitasse and the guest is supposed to keep the cup and cover it with her hand to indicate she doesn't want any more. We endured a few rounds of those, before we decided we couldn't take one more sip. The truth is we were getting hungry and bored after more than three hours cooped up on that second floor, talking mostly to each other. We knew that the meal is the last part of a gathering, but the men down below had already been served their "goat grab" and were finishing their dinner, as we had noticed when we peeked through a crack from behind the curtains.

A "goat grab" is one of those (either all male or all female) communal dinners where everyone reaches for the meat first, without any utensils, just their bare hands. It is an impressive thing to watch or to take part in, as my husband and children related to me. It takes two people to carry an enormous tray of food (up to a yard in diameter) to each group of guests. A goat or half a goat, roasted to perfection, occupies the center of the plate, surrounded by white rice spiced with herbs and raisins. Once everyone is seated around the food, the host invites the guests to reach for whatever part of the roast is the closest and start pulling the meat from the carcass. The rice, too, is eaten with the tips of the fingers, making a ball, until all the food is gone and all feel satisfied. There are no individual plates or silverware; this is a communal "fingers only" event. I have heard that if there is a guest of honor he might be offered the eye of the goat, a privilege most foreigners abhor because they simply can not stomach it. Fortunately, most hosts are sensitive to the foreigners' dislike for the prized morsel.

On special occasions, such as weddings, men wearing daggers and swords around their waist get in a circle and dance and shout holding their swords high, while the other men around them keep the beat with a rhythmic clapping. Those dances as well as the ceremony of passing around a vessel with burning incense for the guests to waif are interesting experiences the foreign male guests get to enjoy; women don't take part in any way in such events.

When the women upstairs were finally served at around four in the afternoon, Robin and I were famished (We had not eaten anything since breakfast that morning.) The food didn't look particularly attractive (the meat had been taken off the bones and piled in the center of the tray with rice on the sides), and it was cold. As eating started in earnest, Robin said she was not going to eat everybody's saliva, or without a plate and a fork, and walked away disgusted. The tall, husky Texan could not take any more Arab hospitality. I took it more philosophically, since I had seen enough cultural differences in other places (mostly in Africa and Iran) not to blame the hosts in situations like this one. Goat meat is not my favorite meat, and this one was a little bit too fat and cold, but the rice was very good and I ate my fill of it with my fingers without any trouble; after all, years before I had eaten fried caterpillars in the Congo without offending my hosts or making a fuss over it.

Right after eating I thanked the hostess and went downstairs to join my family. We had learned that leaving right after a meal is within proper etiquette in Saudi Arabia, so it was time to gather the family and leave. Robin had joined her husband and complained about the whole thing. He managed to get her a plate of food with fork and knife to use.

It is strange, but on returning to the United States in July 1983, my family experienced cultural shock in reverse. After two years of sheltered life in Saudi Arabia, our sons, then 14 and 9-years old, were overwhelmed by the amount of crime reported in the news from San Antonio (Texas), and nationwide, and felt that they had to be more on guard and less trusting of other people in their own country than they had been in a foreign land. In the first few weeks they even proposed that we sell our house and go back to Saudi Arabia, or to Spain, where they had seen a more tranquil and secure way of life. Little by little we all readjusted to life in Texas. We were to face a similar letdown in 1992 when we returned to San Antonio after living two years in Indonesia.

A few months before leaving Saudi Arabia in July '83, my husband and I realized one of our dearest dreams, to go to India and sit at the feet of a great saint. The visit to this holy man I will describe later under the chapter "Gurus and Masters" and "A Visit to a Living Saint."

## Chapter 4

# In and out of Africa

Dealing with life-threatening asthma is not new to me. At age 28, shortly after the birth of my first child in Feb. of '69, I developed some allergies that became progressively worse within the next year.

Debts brought about by the baby's birth (an unexpected cesarean) plus an operation for pyloric stenosis the baby developed at age three weeks, were a great burden on us. We had no medical insurance, since my husband's teaching position at the Defense Language Institute at Lackland AFB in San Antonio, Texas was at that time only "temporary." In view of our precarious financial situation, we decided to volunteer for a two-year assignment overseas. I am sure our youth and our love for travel and adventure also played a role in our decision to apply for an assignment that most teachers at DLI would not even have considered. One-year teaching assignments (unaccompanied) were also available for Vietnam, but leaving wife and baby was not an option for my husband and, besides, we were against the war. So, we went to the Congo[4] instead.

We arrived in the capital, Kinshasa, on April 22, 1970 with Eric, our one-year-old baby, on a two-year teaching assignment.

The cultural shock didn't affect me too much, but the climate did, almost immediately. Lack of sanitation, a humid

---

[4] *The country of Zaire was known at that time as the Republique Democratique du Congo. It was named Zaire in 1971. As I finish these pages in June 1997, Zaire is changing government for the first time in more than thirty years and is being renamed Republic Democratique du Congo.*

and unhealthy climate, mosquitoes, flies, parasites, etc. made our lives rather difficult in Kinshasa, especially with a baby to take care of in this kind of environment. The water was not even safe to brush your teeth.

Not that we lived in a dump. The U.S. embassy had provided us and the other member of the English language team and his family with two good size apartments, on the third and fourth floors of a central building, on the main avenue in Kinshasa.

The English language school where they were to teach Congolese military personnel was conveniently located on the second floor of the same building. But there was a constant smell of sewage and rotten garbage coming from the building itself, since garbage was disposed of by sending it down, through chutes from every floor, to the basement of the building. This made our living environment quite unpleasant most of the time. To the smell of garbage that of DDT was added. The city was sprayed weekly by truck and by plane, since mosquitoes and malaria were a fact of life. We still had to take malaria medicine every day, but that didn't guarantee you would be free from the disease; you would just get a milder case. My husband and our son experienced some of the fever and chills typical of malaria.

Fresh vegetables, on the street or in small shops, were rather scarce, sickly in appearance and very expensive. I remember my first visit to a public market in Kinshasa, shortly after our arrival. It was in the open, very muddy after the rain and foul smelling. The source of the smell was the meat: goat meat, elephant meat, monkey meat, etc., all in different states of "dryness"; there were flies everywhere; I never went back there. After a while we started ordering meat, cheese, eggs and fruit from South

Africa every two weeks, through the U.S. embassy. Once in a while the U.S. military plane carrying our food from Johannesburg would be delayed several days and everybody's food would arrive in Kinshasa in a rather unappetizing condition, since the dry ice it was packed in had its limitations.

The U.S. embassy provided a very nice recreation facility outside the city, with swimming pools, tennis courts, restaurant, etc. for all official personnel and their families. It was a good place to go on weekends when defying the crazy traffic was a little bit easier than on weekdays.

A number of good restaurants downtown offered international cuisine at very high prices, but is was good to dine out once in a while. As to the national dishes, we had a chance to try them too. We had a rather memorable experience one day when a Congolese English instructor, a teacher where my husband taught, invited us to his home for dinner. He had asked my husband what we liked to eat, and Cliff had answered that we ate just about everything. Dinner was almost ready when we arrived at monsieur Cappape's house; we met his wife and small children and soon were shown to the dinning room where a buffet had been prepared. There were several interesting looking dishes; some we recognized, others we didn't. The chicken with peanut sauce was quite good; a gruel made from cooked manioc mashed with spices was a new twist on a root vegetable I had grown up with, and so were the green leaves of the manioc plant, prepared as you would spinach, which in Colombia were never used for food and went to waste. Both dishes were tasty and showed me new ways to eat a familiar food. But the dish that stunned us was a bowl of fried grayish grubs. We asked what that was and they answered simply, "chinelle." Not to be impolite, I ate two of them and my husband a few more. They were not bad but the looks of them made me cringe a little. We learned later that "chinelle" (caterpillars) were considered a delicacy in the Congo. Monsieur Cappape probably expected to have a good laugh at our expense, but we acted with all the dignity we could muster. He and his wife visited us once or twice after that, and I saw him a few more times at the school. To me he always looked like a jolly good prankster.

The Congo's official language was French, but dozens of African languages were spoken in the country. Around Kinshasa, the capital, French and Lingala were spoken the most. I love languages; in my youth, in my native Colombia, South America, I had studied several: English and Russian, plus some French, Italian and German. Soon after our arrival in Kinshasa, I started attending French classes twice a week at the American embassy, mostly to pass the time and to distract my mind from the allergies and respiratory problems I was developing. The embassy was located within walking distance from our apartment.

The American community in Kinshasa was badly shaken by a tragic incident around August 1970. One weekend a group of men and women from the embassy had gone on a picnic on the banks of a tributary of the Congo River, outside the capital. One of the men in the group, a Major Bauer (West Point graduate), noticing a hut on the other shore, decided, on impulse, to swim across the river and back. His girlfriend was one of those present. He had swum no more than a quarter of the distance when the group noticed a huge crocodile swimming towards the major. Their screams turned to horror when they saw the animal pull the man down and disappear with him under water. At that point they realized there was nothing they could do for their friend. A search party was organized to look for the officer's remains. A day later they found his torso, which had floated to the bank of the river, but nothing else. Crocodiles are known to hide their prey in a kind of underwater nest for some time before they feed on it. The search party also killed three crocodiles close to the shore that day, one of them acting very aggressive as if trying to defend his catch; it was an old crocodile, over thirteen feet long. We had met Major Bauer at official embassy events such as the Fourth of July celebration and had seen him at the recreation center. My husband had chatted with the major a week earlier while siting next to him at a dinner party. It was a very sad experience for the whole foreign community.

The mighty Congo River, the second longest river in the world, separates the capitals of two neighboring countries: Kinshasa, the capital of the Democratic Republic of the Congo, and Brazzaville the capital of the Popular Republic of the Congo (referred to then as "the communist Congo.") The Brazzaville shore of the river could be seen clearly from the top floor of the apartment building we lived in, since it was located no more than ten blocks from one of the shores.

The climate around the capital, as I said before, was humid all the time and very unhealthy. A lady doctor from Argentina, who lived around the corner from us and whom I consulted a few times, told me she had never seen so many strange illnesses in her practice, and that she wasn't amused at the widespread growth of venereal diseases she was seeing, either. The worst part, she said, was that the common practice of men having sex outside of marriage was bringing those diseases to their wives and through birth to the children. Unfortunately, her bleak observations proved almost prophetic; Zaire, or the Congo as it is called again, has become one of the countries most affected by AIDS in all of Africa.

Health was becoming a big concern for me, too. In the later part of 1970 a case of bronchitis slowly turned into asthma, the severe asthma that has afflicted me ever since. I started to lose weight, coughed constantly and felt short of breath most of the time. By Christmas of 1970 I could barely take care of my little boy. A houseboy (a grumpy old man) helped with the cleaning and did the cooking.

Early in 1971 I was visiting the embassy's medical dispensary once a week. Not seeing much improvement, I also consulted our Argentinean friend and another American doctor who was in charge of one of President Mobutu's private clinics. By mid February, as asthma became worse, the U.S. embassy physician, Dr. Olney, agreed that it was better to medi-vac me as soon as possible to a U.S. military hospital in Frankfurt, Germany, for testing and treatment. He would accompany me, given the risk of trouble during the flight.

I left the baby with a Colombian family with three teenaged daughters, whom I knew would take care of Eric much better than his father and the houseboy could. Fortunately, we had found several Spanish-speaking families, including two from Colombia working for the United Nations in Kinshasa, who were more than willing to render help and encouragement when we needed it the most. This gave me enough peace of mind to leave my baby and go to Germany in search of medical help.

After two weeks in the U.S. Army hospital in Frankfurt, I returned to Kinshasa on March 10 as good as new, only to get sick again in about a week with daily asthma attacks, plus sinus trouble. March 24, 1971, my 30th birthday, I spent most of the day on an examination table, at the U.S. Embassy dispensary, receiving adrenaline shots and intravenous medication to help my breathing.

Less than two weeks after my birthday, I landed in the emergency room of a public hospital in Kinshasa with a severe asthma attack. I remember how embarrassed the nuns were a few times, to have me in a communal room with about twenty more native men and women, the men walking around naked all the time, and the nuns asking me to cover my face. My answer was: "I am too sick to care, and it doesn't offend me in any way." A white man (a Belgian who had been shot in the stomach) and I were the only two white patients at the time in that big hospital room. After two days there, I was transferred to a private hospital in Kinshasa, one so comfortable that my room had an extra bed for someone to stay overnight, and a sitting room with view to a garden for visitors or the patient to rest in.

Although the attention was excellent on the part of the nuns and doctors in both hospitals, there was very little hope for any lasting improvement of my condition as long as I remained in that environment. In April it was decided to medi-vac me to the U.S. on a military flight.

An Air Force C-141 Starlifter, empty of any cargo[5], was provided to fly me and my little son Eric, then two years old, to Charleston, NC and then on to Pensacola, Florida, where my parents-in-law resided. We left Kinshasa May 3,

---

[5] The aircraft's crew chief had ordered that the aircraft not be loaded with cargo due to the life-threatening allergy/asthma I'd been experiencing.

1971. My husband stayed behind in his job, and asked to be sent back to the U.S. as soon as possible.

While flying over west Africa, the C-141 developed mechanical problems that forced us to land in Monrovia, Liberia and wait for a spare part to be sent from the U.S. for the crew to make the repairs. In the meantime, since my condition was not as normal as desired, my little boy and I stayed in a hospital owned by the Firestone Company, located outside Monrovia, close to the company's huge rubber plantation. It was one of the cleanest hospitals I had ever seen anywhere, very unusual for that kind of location and climate; it was sparkling clean, cool and free of bugs of any kind. A nurse told me that by far the most frequent medical treatments rendered there were for malaria and deadly snakebites. She said that having the hospital in the middle of the plantation was of extreme importance when dealing with poisonous snakebites, in which case every minute counts, even though workers in the field might have used their emergency kits. Some of the deadliest snakes in the world live in Africa. In Kinshasa I had heard of one called the "two-step Mamba," probably the deadliest of them all.

After the plane was repaired, we left Monrovia and headed for South Carolina. The progress I had made at the Firestone hospital was upset by the spraying of the inside of the military plane with some kind of pesticide as we were flying past the African continent. I tried to protest, but it was useless. The two medical attendants on board knew this spraying could not be good for an asthmatic or for my little boy, but they did it anyway. Those were the regulations.

Other than that the flight was smooth. After arriving in Charleston, a military medical flight (transport type aircraft with a red cross on it) took us to Pensacola, where my parents-in-law were waiting for us. They were surprised to see how thin and sickly I looked, weighing less than ninety pounds.

Pensacola being a humid climate didn't do much for my condition, but it was a considerable improvement over the unhealthy climate I had been exposed to for more than a year in the Congo, and my in-laws' home was a peaceful and loving place to convalesce. A nose operation to remove polyps and clear the sinus cavities also helped me breath better.

In three months my husband was able to leave Kinshasa and return to his regular post at Lackland AFB. He joined us in July at his parents' home in Pensacola, spent a week there and then, with me and the baby, continued to San Antonio.

## Chapter 5

# Chasing a Cure

Back in Texas, in the months that followed, the asthma did not relent. Almost immediately after our arrival in July 1971, I became a regular visitor to emergency rooms. The treatment for asthma was so harsh, with cortisone and antibiotics among other drugs, I developed a very painful stomach ulcer and had to be hospitalized for that alone once.

Disappointed and with more health troubles than before, I decided to go back to Bogotá, Colombia, where I had lived many years in my youth, healthy and free from allergies. We thought the high altitude of Bogotá (about 10,000 feet), might be beneficial to my health. I would go ahead with our two- year-old son Eric to my mother's home in Bogotá and try other approaches to the problem. If things looked up, my husband would resign his job at Lackland, taking just enough time to get rid of the car and some furniture we wouldn't bother to ship, and travel to Colombia.

My mother and other relatives who lived in Bogotá were very optimistic about me finding the cure I needed, and were very happy to help us. When the baby and I arrived in Bogotá in November 1971, everyone was alarmed to see how skinny and sickly I looked; I weighed as much as when I was 10-years old. My family had not seen me in four years, nor had they seen the baby.

Under my mother's tender loving care and some natural remedies, I showed a quick recovery from the ulcer, and the respiratory troubles became more bearable. After a month and a half, my husband was so encouraged by the news, he quit his job and didn't even bother to sell small things, such as baby furniture; he just left the items with somebody at the apartments where we lived, and traveled to Colombia. He arrived in Bogotá on Christmas Day 1971.

Bogotá is located on a high plateau in the Andean mountains on the northern part of South America; it has a cool and crisp climate year round, with temperatures between 40 and 75 degrees Fahrenheit, and little variation during the wet and dry seasons. With a climate like that every imaginable flower can grow to perfection; in fact most of the flowers Colombia exports to Europe and the United States come from around Bogotá.

In 1971 the city's population was approximately 3.5 million people. Today it is close to 7 million. The city is one of the most important economic and cultural centers in South America, constantly bubbling with growth and activity. From the colonial period many homes and churches have been lovingly preserved or restored. Some of the churches date from the 1600s to the 1700s and are wonderful examples of an intriguing mixture of native, colonial and European Renais-sance and Baroque styles. The exquisitely carved and ornate altars on many of them are truly inspiring to the visitors, whatever their faith. As a young woman in the early sixties, working as a secretary in downtown Bogotá, I used to go across the street to one of these old churches to enjoy a moment of prayer, beauty and relaxation, many, many times. Being away from the Church (its dogma) did not mean being away from God or from taking delight in man's spiritually inspired master-pieces.

Over all, Bogotá is a modern city with all the advantages and problems of a big city. Pollution is very high, and the traffic can be maddening at times.

I had spent many years in Bogotá in my youth, and had lived there continuously for ten years, from my teens until I left Colombia for the United States in 1967, as a newly-wed. Four years later, coming back to my family, and that (for me) perfect climate, was a real joy. By chance we were able to find vacant the same apartment my husband and I had lived in after we got married in 1966. The owner of the building was an old friend of mine and classmate as Russian students years before. The location of her apart-ment building had one of the best views in town, being in the foothills of Mt. Monserrate, one of the several moun-tains that surround the Bogotá plateau.

My husband went back to teaching English at the Centro Colombo-Americano, a U.S. sponsored bi-national center, where he had previously taught English from 1965 to 1967. His salary, however, was very modest by U.S. stan-dards since he was "a local hire," his pay based on the Colombian economy. It was enough to get by reasonably well, but without many luxuries.

Because of his experience teaching foreign military per-sonnel in the U.S., my husband was chosen to teach an English class at the presidential palace in Bogotá to the Colombian officers assigned to President Pastrana, includ-ing his helicopter pilot, his protocol officer and the officer in charge of security; five officers in all, from every branch of the Colombian armed forces. The presidential palace in Bogotá is a place where history and tradition have been kept with pride and grace. President and Mrs. Kennedy were quite impressed with it when they visited Bogotá in 1961. Mrs. Kennedy acknowledged later on a television interview that the sense of history she had observed at the presidential palace in Bogotá, had inspired her to come back to Washington and start a much needed redecoration work in the White House. I never stepped any farther than a waiting room of the Colombian presidential palace, but my husband was given a tour of it by one of his students and was very appreciative of the good taste and relevance of the decor.

Life was pleasant for us in Bogotá, and my health improved considerably, but by the end of the year (1972) the Colombo Americano offered my husband a job, with a higher salary, as director of courses at the bi-national center in Cartagena, on the northern coast of Colombia, and we accepted. The U.S. embassy would pay for our moving expenses, but other than that my husband would continue to earn a peso salary based on the Colombian economy (less than half of what he was making annually at Lackland two years earlier).

Cartagena was founded by the Spaniards in 1533 and is located on the northwestern coast of Colombia. The port city of Cartagena became an important center to the Spanish *conquistadores* for launching expeditions and especially for shipping the gold and emeralds so abundant in the interior of Colombia, as well as the gold and silver from the entire New Granada colony (formed by what is presently Colombia, Ecuador and Venezuela). But the vessels and galleons that took the treasures to Spain did not always make it to their destination, and many of them sank in stormy weather or were sunk by pirates in the

Caribbean, not far from Florida. In recent years treasures worth hundreds of millions of dollars have been recovered from the waters around Florida by divers looking for such sunken treasure.

So busy and rich was Cartagena that pirates from France and England soon infested the Caribbean looking for vessels carrying treasure. The city had to be defended at all cost and Spain brought her best engineers to build fortifications around the city and the bay. Slaves were brought from Africa to do most of the work, which started in 1586. Thus the largest work of military architecture in the New World was created in the sixteenth century to defend Cartagena. But the city was not invulnerable; Sir Francis Drake, the Baron de Pointis and the much feared Robert Baal captured and sacked the city not long after its fortification had began. Later, however, Cartagena resisted many attacks, including one long siege in 1741 by the English fleet under Admiral Edward Vernon. (As a matter of fact, George Washington's residence on the Potomac River was named "Mount Vernon," in honor of this admiral, by the president's brother Lawrence, who built the mansion and had served in the British navy under Vernon. George Washington inherited Mount Vernon in 1752.)

Today, hundreds of thousands of tourists from all over the world come to Cartagena and are charmed by the castles, forts and walls around the oldest part of the town and by the natural beauty of this gracious city. A balmy climate year round makes the place even more enticing. That is exactly why when we were offered a chance to settle there, we took it without hesitation. We figured also that the clean air and salinity from the ocean might help my respiratory troubles.

We found a spacious house, not farther than 150 feet from the beach, in a quiet middle-class neighborhood. Apart from our living quarters, the house had three more rooms, a kitchen and bathroom in the back, separated by a small yard, enough for another family to live in. Rather than having half of the place empty, and also to supplement our income, we sublet the back rooms to three Americans; one was a teacher at the Centro Colombo-Americano, where my husband worked, and the other two, husband and wife, were Peace Corps volunteers. Being so close to the beach, not more than 150 feet, at night we could hear the sound of the waves from our bedroom; a gentle sound to go to sleep with. In the yard behind the apartment and the one between the main house and the apartment, there were a variety of mature fruit trees for us to enjoy. We had bananas, lemons, coconuts, guavas, mangos and sour sop, all very appetizing and plentiful for our small family and friends. A pair of yellow-head Amazon parrots we had brought from Bogotá kept everybody entertained with their boisterous antics; they talked, laughed, cried and whistled all day long. I made it a habit to go to the beach with little Eric every morning and sometimes again in the afternoon when my husband came home from work.

The bi-national center where my husband worked as director of courses had perhaps about 200 students – daytime and evening; it occupied a big two-story restored colonial house, within the walls that surround the old part of town. The house had a squared shape, with balconies all around overlooking an enclosed patio shaded by several trees – a very attractive place, like many in that area. It was rumored that the house had ghosts, but my husband, who spent a few nights there, before I and our household goods arrived from Bogotá, never saw or heard a thing.

Two of my brothers and their families, who lived in the nearby city of Barranquilla, about two hours away, came to visit us often, or we went to their homes, and it was good to be close to them. My mother, too, came from Bogotá in August to spend some time with us. She was quiet, gentle and wise, a widow since 1965. Each of her eight children felt privileged to have her come and stay with them at any time, and her daughters and sons-in-law, too, loved to have her around. She liked being close to the sea and enjoyed going for a daily swim with us and walking on the beach, or just sitting quietly in the yard in a pensive mood.

In regard to my health, Cartagena did not deliver according to our expectations; the progress I had made in Bogotá slowly weakened. I had to visit doctors very often, trying also a few faith healers and herb specialists in between. Nothing did much good, but, at any rate, I was grateful that I had not needed hospitalization or emergency care since I had left San Antonio in December 1971; that alone was an improvement of sorts.

I started to rely more heavily on prayer; mine and my family's prayers especially. When we heard that some group in town was teaching and practicing yoga meditation, my husband and I welcomed the opportunity to learn about it. We attended an introductory lecture on spiritual yoga practices, as taught by Guru Maharaji, the boy guru from India that was causing a sensation in the U.S. and elsewhere in the western world. Liking what we heard, and being the only such group that we were aware of in town, we soon became regular attendants at the meetings that Maharaji's followers held weekly in downtown Cartagena.

About this period of spiritual growth, I will tell a little more in the chapter entitled "Gurus and Masters."

## Chapter 6

# A Birth Announcement

One evening, around the middle of 1973, while meditating at home, in Cartagena, I had a strange vision. In the darkness of my closed eyes there appeared a pink human fetus, well defined already, with its head bent and hands together like in prayer. The fetus was surrounded by golden-yellow light; it stayed in view a few seconds and then faded.

After I finished my meditation and my husband ended his, I told him about what I had just seen while meditating. We thought it was odd, and we soon forgot about it. But, four weeks later, when I missed my period, we realized my vision had been an announcement, just prior to conception, we were sure, since my periods were so regular. We were very moved, and surprised. Our son Eric was four-years-old, and we had not been planning on having any more children because of my health problems. This new baby had not been in our plans, but it was welcomed nevertheless.

The pregnancy itself was a gentle one, but the asthma, allergies and an occasional bronchitis, without the benefit of drugs such as cortisone and antibiotics, which I couldn't take during the first months, made it extremely hard; my bouts of sneezing, alone, made me fear several times I could lose the baby, but he held on tight.

With a new baby on the way, my health not doing well, and financially in poor shape, we decided it was time to go back to the United States and look for a better paying job overseas, probably in the Middle East.

I was four months pregnant when we left Cartagena for Florida, on a small freighter, in November 1973. The boat was empty of cargo except for an extra deck tank of fuel, since it was cheaper to fill up in Colombia, and that meant savings to the owner. We had a nice, big cabin for ourselves, our household goods and our two Amazon parrots. The birds were the first ones to get seasick; it was rather funny to see them throw up, unaccustomed to the pendulum-like movement of the boat. My husband thought it would be interesting to see what the parrots would do if he changed the direction of the swing, by turning their cage half way; which really startled those poor birds, rocking suddenly in a different direction. I was sorry for them, since I had felt seasick, too, almost from the beginning of the trip; so had our little boy Eric. My husband, who knew what to expect from previous short and long trips by boat, had prepared himself well by taking seasickness pills right before the ship started sailing. I thought he was exaggerating the need for medicine, and reminded him I was the pregnant passenger, more likely to get nauseous than he was.

We encountered rough seas after the second day of sailing. One morning we woke up to the news that the storm had broken loose the extra tank of fuel the boat was carrying, spilling it, and had done some other damage, though not serious. The crew had been very busy for hours. Mercifully we had slept soundly through the emergency. The bad weather didn't last long, and after seven days at sea, we arrived in Tampa, Florida. There we rented a small truck and headed for Pensacola, where my parents-in-law resided.

An overseas job my husband had applied for came through faster than we had anticipated, giving us just a few weeks to get ready to travel to Iran. My husband would be teaching English to Iranian military personnel in Tehran. We had to sell our beautiful talking parrots that for two years had made our lives so much fun.

## Chapter 7

# Life in Iran

On route to Iran, we spent Christmas and the last week of 1973 in a small town in Germany (Heppenheim, not far from Frankfurt), continuing on to Tehran on New Year's Eve. January 1st was not a holiday in Iran (their New Year begins in March), so downtown Tehran looked very busy that day, the streets full of people and vehicles. From our hotel window that January first 1974, I noticed something very unusual in the streets below: Many of the women on the street were covered from head to toe with what seemed like full length capes, some black, some white. I thought that was a lot of "catholic nuns" for a Muslim country.

That piece of clothing was the "chador," a sign of modesty for Muslim women. I had failed to learn in advance about the women's dress code. I had expected to see just their faces covered with a veil in some fashion, but not their entire bodies. Later someone told me that only the most religious women wore the chador. And sure enough on the streets of Tehran you could see a great contrast in women's attire; it ranged from the miniskirt, hot pants, slacks and long dresses, to the full covering of the chador.

When working overseas for the U.S. government before, we had had a house waiting for us and everything ready for us to move in as soon as we arrived at the new location. This time, working for a private company, we were to find our own house and furnish it according to the allowance we were given. Hotel accommodations were limited to 30 days, so on that account alone it was imperative to get out and start searching for a house as soon as possible. Here I was, five months pregnant, sickly with daily asthma, with a 5-year-old child, and not knowing a word of Farsi, the Iranian language. My husband, of course, was gone all day and very busy at his new job, so it was up to me to take care of our getting settled.

I was not too worried, though. I contacted the United Nations, as I had done before while living in the Congo, and asked for Spanish speaking members. I was overjoyed to hear that there were some agronomists and administrators from Latin America (including one from Colombia), working for the UN and living in Tehran with their families. Through these contacts I learned there were also a good number of Latin American women married to Iranians that I could get in touch with. My country did not have diplomatic relations with Iran at that time. The closest Colombian embassy was in Beirut, Lebanon.

Two Colombians married to Iranian men, and longtime residents in Tehran, an Iranian lady married to an American and a Colombian married to an American were wonderfully helpful to us. In a short time we found an apartment in a nice part of town, quite expensive, without heat and completely bare, all of that not uncommon in Tehran in the 1970s. Fortunately, the company my husband was working for subsidized most of the rent. If you have lived overseas, you know that bargaining for everything, from vegetables to refrigerators, is a way of life and that it is expected of everyone. Knowing the language and customs of the country, my new friends and I did a very fine job furnishing the apartment with the available money, and my family was able to settle down with relative ease. More importantly, my friends were very helpful in recommending an English speaking obstetrician, a pediatrician and a hospital they trusted. What a team we made! I think we women are so well gifted in dealing with these things.

Some time later I, in turn, was able to help another pregnant newcomer, a Colombian married to an Italian, find her way around Tehran, introduce her to my doctors and translate for her during her first two visits to the obstetrician, since she did not speak much English (just Spanish, Italian and French.) On the second visit we discovered the doctor spoke French, too. French was the preferred foreign language of cultured Iranians, and my fair knowledge of it came very handy on several occasions, when English or my rudimentary Farsi failed to do the job of communicating.

Our son Christopher John was born three months after our arrival, on April 1, 1974, at Tehran General Hospital. He wasn't expected for another month and the doctor was planning on performing a cesarean two weeks before the due date, but my poor health must have caused my early delivery. The baby weighed exactly seven pounds, was very sweet and seemed to be in good health, showing no signs of cortisone deficiency as the doctor had anticipated.

The baby moved me in a strange way. It was not only a great love this little one inspired in me, but also a sense of respect and admiration; feelings other than just the maternal love, which I had known with my first born, Eric. It was more like the joyful feeling of greeting a long-time-absent dear old friend.

Christopher was not as healthy as we thought. He was just a few weeks old when we noticed he was vomiting very often, right after eating, like his brother had done five years earlier. Pyloric stenosis is more common in first-born males than in second-born males, but this baby, like his brother, had the condition, too. Surgery could have relieved it, but we were afraid to have it done in Iran. So, we opted instead for treating him with a muscle relaxant, which helped a little. For a year and a half the baby threw up at least once a day, becoming somewhat malnourished. I tried giving him nourishing soups made with a little meat, grains, vegetables and milk, to compensate for the feedings he couldn't utilize well. With great patience and loving care the baby survived without surgery. Other than that Christopher was a fine, very sweet and loving baby with beautiful dark eyes that were the focus of admiring looks and compliments from friends and strangers. That, in Persia, where people are noted for their beautiful eyes.

Tehran in the mid-seventies was a city of approximately four million people, and, as in most developing countries, the capital showed marked contrasts in the education, affluence and status of its dwellers. There was great wealth in some sections of the city and bleak conditions in other parts of the same city; there were streets in residential areas where the "wheeler-dealers" lived, lined with Mercedes Benzes and other expensive cars, while in the south of the city, for example, the poor and newly arrived villagers still lived in primitive conditions and goats and camels were more visible than cars, with the humble business of selling manure for heating and fertilizing alive and well. Tehran has harsh winters and heating is essential. Those who could not afford kerosene for heating made do with burning dried dung.

The kerosene heaters used in most homes and many businesses that did not have central heating created the worst pollution I have ever seen. We had two in our home for two years, until the landlord changed to a central system (still using kerosene). Greasy soot, a byproduct of combustion, stuck to walls, curtains and furniture in the house. Worst of all it clung to one's nose and lungs, a real menace for asthmatics like me. The winter months were dreadful in this respect, but, with temperatures below freezing, we needed the heat. To make matters worse the city was surrounded by mountains that acted like a bowl to keep the fumes and pollution trapped inside; a yellowish haze was constantly present.

The traffic was a real nightmare for everyone; it was madness in motion. You could not even feel safe on the sidewalks, since motorcyclists and bikers would have no qualms about riding on the sidewalks among pedestrians in order to get to their destination, or just to get ahead. Traffic signals and police did not mean much to drivers and were of little help to the frustrated humans on foot, as well; crossing a main street was an act of courage, and it was done at your own risk; fender benders, and more serious accidents, too, were a way of life. My husband and I would sometimes make a bet and walk some of the streets around our house counting how many of the cars parked along them were not dented. Hardly any of them were; most were dented in various ways and degrees. We of course, never gave it a thought to own a car in Tehran. My husband rode a company bus to and from work and didn't have to worry about driving. Taxis were very affordable to rent by the hour, plus there were thousands of collective taxis going around the city. Collective meant that the taxis would stop to pick up anybody along a certain general direction, until they filled up the car; all you had to do was shout the name of the intersection you needed to get off at. This system worked remarkably well.

Riding public buses I was able to explore many nooks and crannies of Tehran in the following three years, without a single unpleasant incident. One thing I had to my advantage, that many foreigners didn't have, was the fact that I looked as Iranian as the next person's sister and it was the same thing for my two children with their dark eyes and dark hair. Countless times I was stopped in the streets by Iranians asking for directions. The funny thing is that some of them thought I really was an Iranian trying to pass as a foreigner.

Foreign women, the blond type, were not as lucky as I was getting around without attracting unwanted attention. Iranian men sometimes displayed a sick curiosity towards blond foreigners through the ugly and vulgar acts of grabbing those women in the street, or exposing themselves in front of the ladies. A Canadian neighbor of mine was once surprised by an Iranian officer who lived on her same street, when one day, as she walked to the corner store, he called from his parked car: "Madam, Madam!" and then proceeded to show her his genitals. She couldn't believe this was coming from a neighbor, and a military officer at that. Another young woman I knew, had been harassed a few times and had had one breast grabbed and twisted while walking on a busy street. There were other horror stories of that sort circulating among the foreign community. One woman, for example, had met with laughter, even from a policeman, when she had screamed for help while being attacked in the street. Only seeing her throw up in disgust, made her attacker stop. Invariably the only thing in common in these attacks was that the victims were foreign and blond. On the other hand, a woman walking with a child was usually left unmolested.

Of course, not all Iranian men were perverts, but there was a noticeable immaturity in their behavior in many everyday situations. Cheating on people's checks in restaurants and overcharging on taxi fares was a daily occurrence. As for waiters in restaurants and hotels, we had never seen any nastier service than that; they would just about beat you up in some of those places. Iranian women, on the contrary, seemed to be full of character and good sense. Those qualities, I was told by foreign women married to Iranians, made Iranian women the real strength of the family.

To be fair, Iran did have some unique and wonderful things to show the world. Their art, their carpets, their music, their language, were all very beautiful to me.

Iranian food was one of the most varied, imaginative and colorful I have ever tasted. Their knack for using fruit and nuts, from green to full ripeness, fresh or dried, in cooking, jams, sauces and drinks, was most unusual and always delicious. Being invited to a home was a treat to the palate and the eyes; you wished you had a movie camera on those occasions to capture the beautiful array of dishes. Bread, in many different shapes and thickness, including one paper-thin, was made and sold hot in little shops three times a day. Yogurt, the national food, was sold in every corner store by the bucket, a nutritious, refreshing, pure product from goats' milk; my family and I took to it like ducks to water. One American woman who had lived in Tehran for some time already, asked me one day what it was that she had seen me and many people carry in a bucket so often. I told her it was yogurt and encouraged her to try it. I made soups, curries, sauces, gelatin, deserts, etc. with it.

A typical everyday meal for workers on the street during their lunch break (I observed many construction workers near our house and other people at the open market), was made up of fresh bread, raw onions, goat's cheese and yogurt; a highly nutritious meal, in my view, for anybody, rich or poor.

## Chapter 8

# The Magic of Carpets

Westerners living in Iran were almost expected to take an interest in carpets, and I am sure most of us did; it was hard to resist their magical "web." I remember how our landlord kept asking us when we were going to buy a carpet. He couldn't imagine that it really wasn't any trouble for us to walk on bare floors. Actually, the floors in our apartment were marble and quite attractive by themselves.

Our introduction to Persian carpets was unusual. After we arrived in Tehran we started noticing that carpet shops would place a carpet or two on the sidewalk in front of the store. We thought it very inconvenient for the pedestrian to have to take the street in order to avoid stepping on the carpets, until we noticed that everybody else was walking on them. Then we noticed more carpets on the street, and the traffic just rolling on them. When I later asked a shopkeeper at a shop near our home why that was done, he told me it was to speed the aging of the rugs, and added that carpets were not "sissy stuff." Needless to say, right then I decided to learn more about Persian rugs.

I heard from other foreigners that some of the bigger carpet shops in downtown Tehran gave "tours" and informal lectures about their wares every Friday (equivalent in Muslim countries to our Sunday.)

The subject was fascinating and extensive. We learned that not only sheep's wool but also goat's and camel's wool and silk were used in making rugs; about the dyes and processes of dyeing the wool; the weft and warp that held the knots and how the knots were tied; the designs and motifs characteristic to each carpet-producing region of Iran; the time it took one weaver or a team to complete a carpet (from months to years, depending of the density of knots per square inch and the size of the rug, since knots have to be tied one at the time), etc. We also heard that women and children, because of their more delicate hands, were considered the best weavers (not to mention the cheapest).

The audience, sitting atop a flat pile of beautiful rugs, would listen to all that interesting information given by the store's experts, while snacking on bread, goat's cheese and hot tea. (What a non-pressure, yet effective, way to sell rugs that was! And sales they made.) The best part of the show was to view and examine dozens of carpets, from the moderately priced to the very expensive (I touched a few that were priced higher than a fancy Mercedes Benz, but there were some even more expensive than that.). I liked the whole experience so much that I went back a few times and even got my husband to attend those gatherings with me once or twice.

Iranian carpets are the finest in the world. What makes them so? The quality of the materials, the sturdiness of the knot, the number of knots per square inch and the delicacy and detail of the design. The number of knots ranges from 150 or 300 knots for a good looking tribal carpet, to up to 600 knots per square inch for the finest wool and silk rugs. As a way of comparison, handmade Chinese carpets, for example, have a very low density of knots, 30 to 60 per square inch.

Commercial banks in Iran would take your carpet as collateral and grant you a loan on the spot. Banks would also store your carpet if you had to leave your home for a period of time; this service was a necessity since thieves were very discriminating in their pickings and would not think of stealing a television set or anything of that sort if there were rugs around. The carpets in some homes were more expensive than the house itself. Rugs on the floor were not only the pride of the homeowner but a sound investment, since carpets appreciate as they get older. To be considered old, a carpet must be at least a hundred years old.

I ended up buying five modestly priced tribal carpets, of which I still have four, folded up in a closet. With the kind of asthma and allergies I have had for the past twenty-seven years, we must keep the floors in our house completely bare. My children might one day own them when they get their own home.

## Chapter 9

# The Splendors of Persia

The following historical overview may be of interest to the reader.

Iranians are heirs to the Persian Civilization of biblical and post-biblical fame, one of the most magnificent of ancient civilizations. Settled by Aryan tribes around 1500 BC, they became known as the Persian Empire under Cyrus the Great in the sixth century BC, after his conquest of Lydia (546 BC) and Babylon (539 BC). A year after the fall of Babylon, Cyrus freed the great number of Jews that King Nebuchadnezzar II had enslaved almost fifty years earlier (587 BC) after conquering and destroying the kingdom of Judah. Cyrus the Great allowed the Jews to go back to Judea and encouraged them to rebuild the city of Jerusalem, which had been burned to the ground by the Babylonian armies of Nebuchadnezzar II. The magnanimous Cyrus also ordered restitution to the Jews of their wealth and the return of the gold and silver vessels the Babylonians had taken from Jerusalem. But Judea, like the neighboring kingdoms, was to remain tributary to the Persian Empire. In matters of religion Cyrus the Great showed exemplary tolerance towards the conquered peoples, allowing them to worship in their traditional faiths. The Jews remained under the Persian Empire until Alexander the Great defeated the Persians in 331 BC and Judea became a province under Macedonian rule. Later, with the Roman invasion of 47 BC, Judea became part of the Roman Empire.

Cambyses II (ruled 529-522 B.C.), succeeded his father Cyrus the Great. He conquered Egypt and Lybia and crowned himself as Pharaoh, expanding further the empire. Unlike his father, Cambyses was a cruel despot who, wanting absolute control over the empire, did not hesitate to have his younger brother Smerdis murdered. While in Egypt a usurper seized the throne of Persia. On his way back to regain the throne, Cambyses died in 522 B.C.

Darius I, the Great, (521-486 B.C.) succeeded Cambyses II. He conquered India, Macedonia and Thracia. During his reign the vast Persian Empire extended from the Indus River in India to the eastern part of today's Greece. The empire's population was about 40 million.

Darius the Great founded Persepolis as the new capital of the empire, mostly as a ceremonial and religious capital, since the king preferred to have his residence in Susa, which had easier access to the Persian Gulf. The best architects and artists of the age were brought from far and near to build the new capital. Under Darius, Zoroastrianism[6], was proclaimed the official religion of the empire.

Of the magnificent palaces Darius and his two immediate successors built in Persepolis (in what is known today as Esfahan), forty enormous columns, measuring 20 meters (70 feet) in height each, stand today among the vast ruins, along with royal tombs, some terraces and stairways, plus the impressive, bigger than life bas-reliefs showing kings from the conquered nations paying tribute to Darius the Great.

Successive wars against Greece and rebellion in some of the conquered lands, Egypt among them, slowly weakened the Persian Empire after Darius's death in 486 BC. The final blow came in 331 BC with the fall of Persia to

---

[6] *Monotheistic faith founded in Persia by Zoroaster in the seventh century B.C.*

Alexander the Great. The capital, Persepolis, the pride of the Persian Empire, was burned by the Macedonian conqueror. Darius III, King of the Persians, was put to death by Alexander without mercy.

During the early Christian era, the Persians were able to repel the advance of Rome for more than three hundred years, but in the fifth century the Christian religion emanating from the Byzantine Empire managed to reach Armenia and even the heart of Persia, causing many clashes with the followers of the thousand year-old Zoroastrian faith.

The Arabs invaded Persia in the seventh century, and, under their great zeal, Zoroastrianism was gradually replaced by Islam.[7] The Persians found attractive the simplicity of the new faith and its directness, in comparison to the ritualistic character of Zoroastrianism and Christianity in which the intervention of priests was required.

Building mosques for prayer and worship became a necessity in the newly converted lands. Since Islam prohibits the representation of the human figure, the sculpture, bronze work and bas-relief at which the Persians excelled, was practically abandoned; instead, their talents were put to good use in erecting mosques of awesome beauty. A distinctive Middle Eastern style of religious architecture flourished, namely the characteristic arches, onion-shaped domes, intricate mosaic work, and tall and slender minarets. The most perfect example of Islamic architecture is, of course, the Taj Mahal in Agra, India, but there are dozens of Medieval Islamic architectural jewels in Iran alone. Spain, which was for eight centuries the best known center of Islamic culture in the West, has also preserved several wonderful examples of Islamic architecture,

---

[7] *The word Islam means "surrender to the will of God."*

among them the mosque in Cordoba and the great palace of the Alhambra in Granada.

During the three years that I lived in Iran, I greatly admired the beauty of many of the mosques. The exquisite mosaic work covering the whole exterior of some of them was as elaborate as the patterns in the richest Persian rugs. The generous use of turquoise blue in the exterior decoration of the mosques, including the domes, made them appear as bright as jewels.

Talking about jewels, viewing the Crown Jewels of Iran, second only to those of the English Crown, was a memorable experience. The bejeweled vessels and thrones and some ancient crowns in the collection were impressive, as well as some of the modern pieces, including Empress Farah's crown.

The empress was a devoted patroness of the arts. Museums and old palaces were kept in top shape for the enjoyment of Iranians and foreigners alike. Gulistan Palace in Tehran, with its beautiful mirror work that covered the walls and ceilings of many of its rooms, and its marble floor and splendid carpets, was to me a dreamlike place like no other. It brought back to my mind childhood fantasies of what an enchanted palace ought to look like. I enjoyed two or three visits to that place most thoroughly.

In the Middle Ages the Muslims gave the world a tremendous push with their rapid expansion towards Asia, Africa and Europe from the seventh century on. The Arabs knew Egypt and Persia to be great depositories of art and knowledge, and took upon themselves the task of translating both ancient and current texts into Arabic. Knowledge and manuscripts on art, architecture, mathematics, astronomy and medicine were brought by the Arabs to Spain, thus allowing Europe to partake of this knowledge and come out of the dark ages it had groveled in for centuries. Poetry and mysticism from the East were two other delicate and precious gifts brought to Europe by the dynamic and eclectic Muslim invaders.

In the twentieth century, Russia, England and the United States have competed for and exerted considerable influence, at different times, in the political and economic development of oil-rich Persia. A constitutional monarchy had been established in 1906 but still Russian troops occupied parts of the country time and time again. Reza Shah Palahvi (elected Shah in 1925) began to introduce western methods of transportation and communication to a society still living in the Middle Ages. In an effort to speed modernization and to rearrange the political and social structures, the name of the country was changed to Iran in 1935. Women, who for centuries had worn the veil, were ordered to uncover their faces and men to change their traditional attire and head dress for a more western-type style. These drastic changes were opposed by the Muslim hierarchy, causing some bloody confrontations in the streets, but they began to slowly take root.

During World War II the Russian and the British occupied Iran and forced Reza Shah Palahvi to abdicate in favor of his son Mohammed Reza in 1941. After the war the new Shah tried to implement an agrarian reform, distributing privately owned and royal lands among the peasants, but an assassination attempt in 1953, instigated by communist and nationalist factions, in which he was wounded, forced him briefly into exile. Assured of support by the United States, the Shah returned to Iran soon after. Among his goals was to gain recognition for his country and himself as leaders in the Middle East, and this he achieved in record time, aided no doubt by the immense oil resources of Iran.

In the 1960s and 1970s hundreds of thousands of foreigners flocked to Iran to partake of the oil bonanza, among them my English teacher husband and our small family.

But perhaps progress was going too fast for the Iranians and especially for its religious leadership. Underneath their fast growing wealth, confusion, greed, discontent and resentment against foreigners was brewing, which is usually the case when prosperity bypasses the lower crusts of society, while the upper crust becomes rich in a hurry. The presence of foreigners and foreign companies was resented by the masses, who felt the influx of newcomers was driving prices up, out of control. Acts of terrorism against foreign companies and individuals were not uncommon in the 70s. Americans were the main targets of these attacks, but not exclusively. During 1974 to 1976 when we lived in Tehran, for example, American military advisors, were being assassinated at a rate of four a year, a fact both governments tried to keep as little known as possible. As a result, most foreigners in Iran at that time were very concerned and cautious about their movements. The Iranian government was trying to keep rebellious factions at bay. The Shah and his feared secret police (the Savak) for years had kept the prisons full of dissenters, but little by little they seemed to be losing control of the situation. There was a degree of uneasiness and anxiety among the foreign community when we left Tehran for good in December 1976.

From his exile in Iraq and later in France the Ayatollah Khomeini had been plotting for years against the Shah's regime, which he considered anti-Islamic. An uprising, instigated by the Ayatollah against the government, was brutally crushed in December 1978. This incident fanned the revolutionary fires among the masses, which culminated with the fall and abdication of Reza Shah Palahvi in February 1979 and the prompt return of Khomeini to Iran to lead the new Islamic government.

The fateful grounds of the American Embassy in Tehran, where 52 U.S. citizens were held hostage for 444 days, after the Shah's fall, by fanatical Muslims with the acquiescence of their government, were quite familiar to us even though my husband was not in Iran in an official capacity but with a private company. We had been there to register the birth of our son Christopher, to get him a passport, to get my visa for re-entry to the United States, and to celebrate the Fourth of July twice in the three years we lived in Iran.

One of those Fourth of July celebrations featured as special guests a large group of Filipino nationals. (The Philippines achieved its independence from the United States July 4, 1946.) The irony was that the honored guests were kept busy cooking, serving and entertaining the crowd (a Filipino live band, singers, fire eaters, dancers, etc. made up the show) just as in the old days, instead of being treated as guests in the real sense of the word. No wonder the "joint celebration" didn't become a tradition. Another blatant lack of sensitivity that we observed, this time towards the host country, was the fact that large pigs were being roasted, rotisserie style, on the grounds, while the party was being watched by Iranians from the windows and rooftops[8] of surrounding buildings, attracted in part by the loud music. Eating pork is forbidden for Muslims, and

---

[8] *Most houses and buildings in Tehran had flat rooftops. During the summer months many people all over town slept in the open air on those rooftops.*

displaying the whole animal for the neighbors to see must have offended a number of them. Not respecting the customs of your host country can earn you at least a bad reputation.

Foreign companies and individuals who didn't get out of Iran in time (prior to the Khomeini takeover), suffered considerable losses. A friend I corresponded with told me later that two mutual friends, who had renewed their contracts with their company and stayed behind, had been very lucky to get out of Tehran alive with just the clothes on their backs in early 1979. Of all their possessions, what one of the families missed the most were their beautiful Persian rugs, my friend said.

I remember how anxious my husband and I were when my exit visa, issued by the Iranian government, was delayed about two weeks over the expected date of departure. The company had put as in a good hotel and all expenses were being paid, but we simply didn't want to stay in Tehran one day longer. It was a great relief when we finally left for the United States via Moscow and London, quite opposite the feelings we would have some years later when leaving Saudi Arabia and Indonesia, which we did reluctantly.

## Chapter 10

# Of Gurus and Masters

As I said in a preceding chapter, while living in Cartagena, my husband and I had gotten acquainted with the Divine Light Mission, a spiritual movement headed by Guru Maharaji, the boy guru from India, who had based his Mission in the United States and was attracting a strong following along the Americas, as well as in Europe. We became regular attendants to meditation and satsanga[9] sessions and received formal initiation from an Indian Mahatma, a personal delegate of Maharaji, during his 1973 South American tour to impart "knowledge," as they called it, to new aspirants. What this "knowledge" consisted of was some specific meditation techniques, to make meditation more effective. We were encouraged to practice individual and group Raja[10] Yoga meditation, which we did daily until we left Colombia in November 1973, for the United States, in route to the new job in Iran.

We found some of Maharaji's followers in Iran in 1974 and met with them several times for group meditation and fellowship; we even met the same Mahatma there and received from him a second initiation. Most of the devotees, like those in Cartagena, were good people and sincere devotees. But there was among them a pesky Iranian who kept trying to convince us to let him move in with us, calling

---

[9] From the Sanskrit, meaning to sit in the company of God-minded persons to listen to a God-inspired talk. (From "Translations by Baba", compiled by Homer S. Youngs. Sathya Sai Education Foundation. Whitefield, India 1975).

[10] Royal. Thus, Raja Yoga is called "the Royal Road" to God. (From "Translations by Baba").

us on the phone, and even dropping by our house uninvited several times. The man didn't speak much English but communicated in German, driving my husband nuts with all his bellyaching about his family, the government, the environment, the world, etc. He had also come to the conclusion that all the problems of Tehran were caused by "schmutzige Luft" (dirty air), and on this point I tended to agree with him. But it was obvious, from much of his conversation and odd behavior, that he had mental problems. We finally had to tell him to stop bothering us, and as a consequence we started losing interest in attending meetings.

Later in 1974 we heard of the existence in India of a great teacher, considered by many an Avatar, from Bill Millward, a former U.S. navy lieutenant commander who had traveled in India in search of enlightenment prior to coming to Iran. He had spent two years in search of a Guru[11], lived in a few ashrams, practiced Buddhist and Yoga meditation, seen some holy men, and sat at their feet expecting great words of wisdom, all of that with mixed results, mostly positive.

According to Millward, Sathya Sai Baba was already one of the best known spiritual teachers in India, with followers in the millions, including thousands from all corners of the world. This unassuming master was already well-known for his efforts to extend education to the young through his many schools and colleges in the South of India. Millward had seen Sai Baba perform miracles in front of thousands of people, not as a showman would, with theatrical fanfare, he explained, but by the quiet and unexpected materialization of objects of all sizes and "holy

---

[11] *Sanskrit word for teacher, in this case one who guides to spiritual liberation. "Gu" means darkness or ignorance and "ru" stands for its removal thereof. ("Translations by Baba," compiled by Homer S. Youngs. Whitefield, India 1975).*

ash" for the believers to keep and for the unbelievers to wonder. All this was done by just a waving of his hand in the air. We thought we would like very much to go see this man of miracles, but traveling to India with small children was not an advisable thing to do at that time. Our wish, however, would become a reality for us about ten years later, in 1983, while living in Saudi Arabia.

After spending three years in Iran, we returned to Pensacola in time to enjoy Christmas 1976 with my parents-in-law, and have a short vacation in Gulf Breeze. We had saved about seventeen thousand dollars, but didn't have any definite plans as to what to do next. In less than a month my husband had landed another job in the Middle East, this time with Lockheed Aircraft, to teach English in Dhahran, Saudi Arabia, but he would have to start immediately. That meant I would have to stay behind with the children until housing became available for us at his new post, which according to the company, would take no more than two months.

Just before my husband's departure for Saudi Arabia we moved, from the motel on the beach, to a regular apartment in Gulf Breeze, close to an elementary school for seven-year-old Eric to attend.

One day in early 1977, at the apartments' coin-operated laundromat, while doing my laundry, I noticed, among several old magazines left for the customers to read, a small pamphlet advertising the "Autobiography of a Yogi," with the picture of a beautiful man with long hair, as it appears on the front cover of the book. It was Paramahansa Yogananda. As I read the advertisement and looked at the picture, I thought that would be an interesting book to read, and promptly ordered it. As soon as the book arrived I started reading it without delay. What a powerful book it was; every passage rang so true, and so sweet to my heart; those were words from a soul well acquainted with God, I thought. Yogananda's love for God stirred my spirit deeply. Wanting to see more of his teachings, I ordered another of his books plus a cassette recording of one of his lectures.

The first thing I did was listen to the cassette. The strong voice of the master said: "I, Paramahansa Yogananda, am praying with you. Pray with me." I had to stop the tape at this point. Yogananda's voice sounded more familiar and dearer in my mind than my mother's voice. I said, "I know him, I have heard his voice before." But of course, I had not even met the master in this lifetime, since he had died in 1952 when I was eleven years old and living in Colombia. I cried for joy a little while, realizing these were soul memories from long ago.

My sense of hearing and memory for voices is unusually sharp, and it has been so since childhood. One incident that took place in 1966, a short time after I got married, is a good example of that trait. One evening, in Bogotá, I was waiting for my husband at the center where he taught English, sitting on a bench next to two other people I didn't know. Someone stopped by to say hello to one of the persons sitting with me. The voice of the woman next to me, answering the newcomer called my attention. I didn't recognize the face, but her voice was very familiar. I asked her, "Are you so and so?" She said yes, and said she knew me and had passed by me several times but I had ignored her, never wanting to greet her or anything. I apologized and told her I had just recognized her voice a moment before, and mixed in her voice I had also recognized her father's voice. She had been a classmate of mine in my hometown, when we were thirteen. I had not seen her in twelve years. Her father had had a small store in front of the public plaza in our town, and I had talked to him several times in my childhood. He had been dead for a few years, at this time, she told me.

Since 1977 when I "rediscovered" Yogananda's teachings, I have read almost every one of his God-inspired writings, and they never fail to touch my heart. I love and respect many teachers and masters of all the main religions in this world, and I have been blessed to have been in the proximity of one who, for me, is the greatest saint walking this earth at present, Sathya Sai Baba, and I love him deeply. But my guru Paramahansa Yogananda comes first in my heart, very close to God, as no other mortal can. God has sent him to me, time, and time, and time again.

God, the masters, the saints and the angels have ways of communicating with those who love God with all their heart and want him above all things. Unable as I was to meet my guru, in the flesh, this time around, he has come to me twice in my dreams, more real than if I had embraced him in the physical. Those dreams were as follow:

### What do you want?

*Walking a long street, I entered one of the houses, marked at the door with a plaque, like a doctor's office, with the name "Paramahansa Yogananda." I sat down and waited until my name was called. My guru received me in the next room, dressed in white robes and smiling. I knelt at his feet, overcome with emotion, sobbing and calling him "Master, master". He rubbed my head to comfort me, while speaking tender words in several languages, all of which I understood. Then he lifted me by my hands to a standing position and embraced me, while my tears of joy kept flowing. After a moment in his loving arms he asked me "What do you want?" I was still sobbing. Since I didn't answer right away, he called: "Bring the tray with the gifts." Someone brought a tray with several pieces of jewelry on it. The master took a large one, spit on it, then flattened the center of the piece with his fingers and proceeded to place it around my neck. Then he took a bracelet of the same design and repeated the process of spiting and pressing on it, and placed it on my wrist. The two pieces were made of gold, and they fit me perfectly. At the center of each piece there was a rectangle with the silhouette of a leaping man with his arms up, in orange color, on an aquamarine back-ground.* End of the dream.

This dream was so sustaining to my spirit, my whole being felt light and joyful for hours after I woke up; I was-n't even hungry that day. A curious coincidence is that the leaping motion is one I enjoy doing myself in my dreams very often. Leaping and dancing in the air are two recur-ring themes in my dreams.

### A rapturous procession

*In this dream, a group of people was sitting in rows fac-ing my guru, waiting for him to talk. Suddenly the floor of the room opened up and several people dropped into a river running below the room. The floor closed again. Only three people, including myself were left in the room, still silent, facing the guru. Soon after, those who had fallen in the river came back very clean, wearing white robes. Paramahansa Yogananda rose from his seat and signaled everybody to come to the center of the room. Then he threw something like a lasso up in the air and it came down to encircle the group of disciples of about fifty people. It was a giant rosary made of red stones that shone like rubies, and it stood loosely around us at the height of our shoulders. With the guru leading the group we marched, inside the rosary, in reverent procession. I noticed I wasn't walking, but floating along.* End of the dream.

A true guru will love you and guide you throughout millenniums if necessary, until you are "done" spiritually, and can say with him and the masters "My Father and I are one."

## Chapter 11

# A Visit to a Living Saint

In the late 1970s, back in San Antonio, while browsing through books at the bookstore at the metaphysical church we were attending at the time, my husband saw two books next to each other, which attracted his attention. Both had on their cover the figure of an orange-red robed Indian swami with bushy hair, Afro style. My husband recognized immediately the name of the guru he had heard from Bill Millward in Tehran. "That is the man," he thought. We purchased the books and read them. One of them was "Sai Baba Man of Miracles," and the other one was, I think, "The Holy Man and the Psychiatrist." Afterwards we were even more determined to go see this guru.

In 1983, as we were finishing a two-year assignment in Saudi Arabia, the opportunity came for us to go to India to see Sai Baba. In January 1983 we left our sons in Riyadh with a friend and went to India for a two-week visit to Baba's ashram.

Our arrival in Bombay was quite eventful, starting with the surprising news of our need for a visa. I had checked by telephone with the Indian embassy in Jeddah, Saudi Arabia the month before our trip and they had assured me we didn't need one. We panicked momentarily, but then with a quick soulful call for divine help, we stated the purpose of our visit to the immigration officer. He shook his head and said he would have to consult the matter with his superiors. He came back a few minutes later smiling to tell us we had been given a two-week courtesy visa. That was exactly what we wanted. After clearing customs we took a mini-bus to a hotel the driver recommended.

We slept very well at the Atlantic Hotel, on Juhu Beach. The first thing we did the next morning after enjoying a wonderful breakfast was to walk down the beach a while. It was a quiet, fresh and bright morning and the tide had deposited lots of little pink shells on the wet sand. I collected a handful of them while walking, feeling overjoyed and grateful to be in that blessed land of my dreams. I have always loved India and the name alone summons a sweet emotion in my heart every time. I remembered reading in a biography of Mahatma Gandhi that Juhu Beach was one of the places he used to go to rest and convalesce after long periods of work or fasting, late in his life. This beach felt to me like a perfect place for peaceful contemplation and communion with God and nature.

After this refreshing and introspective morning walk, we decided to get back to a main street and see what we could of that part of Bombay before lunchtime. The streets were starting to fill up with traffic and people, the sound of horns from every kind of vehicle, adding to the bustle.

Suddenly, the advance of a funeral procession on one side of the street put a momentary end to the noise and madness. A group of some forty to fifty people walked by in silence and reverence. At the head of the procession a few men rang small bells; then came the body, neatly wrapped in white cloth, covered with loose flowers and carried on a simple stretcher on the shoulders of four men; the rest of the mourners followed. A pyre nearby, probably by the sea, must have been waiting for the incineration of the body. I thought that was a beautiful final rite, simple and dignified too.

What we saw of Bombay that day, mostly from walking around and on our long taxi ride to the airport, and again two weeks later on the stop there on our way back to Saudi Arabia, was a modern, booming city, huge but attractive.

We left for Bangalore that afternoon, and settled in a nice hotel. Making inquiries about how to go to Whitefield, where Baba has his residence part of the year, we found out Baba had just left for Bombay that same day and would be away for four days; our paths must have crossed. At the hotel we met several foreigners staying there who had seen Baba the days and weeks prior to our arrival. They had plans to wait for his return in a few days, and some of them had been coming to India regularly for as many as twenty years to see Baba. They had a lot of anecdotes to tell us. We became well acquainted with "the pink lady," a middle-aged Yoga teacher from Las Vegas, Nevada (always wearing pink saris), her pupil, a young gemologist and sometime Yoga teacher from New Mexico and her boyfriend, on their way to Australia, and a Jewish woman in her 60s, who had come to India to thank Baba in person for a miracle she had received while in a hospital in the United States. She had never heard about Baba at the time, but while being operated on for a serious heart condition, she had seen a man with bushy hair and dark complexion, wearing an orange robe, who assured her she would be well. When she had asked him who he was, he had responded that she would know from a book. Sure enough, some months later, when she least expected it, an employee of hers handed her a book with the picture of Sai Baba on the cover. My husband and I shared a taxi with all of them many times during the following two weeks for daily darshan[12] at Whitefield.

---

[12] *To see a great person; the blessing of seeing a holy one. To see the form of the Lord and receive his blessing. (From "Translations by Baba").*

While waiting for Baba to return, we took advantage of the time to tour the city, which has a lot of historic ruins, beautiful buildings and exquisite gardens (in fact, Bangalore is called "the garden city"), and to do some shopping, something I enjoy anywhere in this world. India is paradise for shoppers. The handicrafts, the silks, the cottons, the carpets and the jewelry were the most attractive things to me, and not too expensive, especially for foreigners.

My husband and I were surprised to see in many stores, on a prominent place, a small shrine for personal worship, showing different Hindu deities and, sometimes, other religions. A few altars had among the pictures of gods and goddesses one of Jesus Christ. But the best example of that curious commingling was the display we saw in one of the taxis we used regularly from the hotel. Its dashboard was decorated with several pictures and symbols of the main religions of the world, including one of Jesus Christ with the words "Smile, Jesus Loves You." Only in India can you catch a sight like that in a public place.

Beggars, many suffering from leprosy, hung around the commercial areas. They would run after the foreigners in groups of up to ten sometimes, begging, and were a bit of a nuisance. You just had to be ready and carry plenty of change in your pocket. In looking at them close up I noticed the women had a fair amount of jewelry on themselves and even their baby girls carried bracelets, anklets and earrings. Except for the very sick and disfigured ones, the beggars look rather dignified in their appearance.

When the awaited day came, and thereafter until the end of our stay, we traveled twice a day, morning and evening, to Whitefield, a small town near Bangalore, to see Baba walk among the thousands of people (hundreds of foreigners among them), who, like us, sat patiently and reverently in the open, in countless rows, men on one side, women on the other, to catch a glimpse of this holy man.

To see Baba move among the rows of devotees touches most people deeply, no matter how many times you have seen him do the same thing. A whole range of emotions flows from your heart, and there is nothing you can do to control it. Sobs and tears flow from men and women, Indian and westerners alike, without shame. I saw some sturdy, middle-aged western men cry openly as Baba approached them; other devotees would try to kiss Baba's feet, while still others had the poise to greet him with bowed head and hands in prayer or hand him a note or a letter. Now and then Baba would pause in front of someone and produce, from the tip of his fingers, holy ashes ("vibuthi"). Those lucky enough to get a little bit of ashes in their cupped hands would immediately lick it with their tongue or rub it on their hands face or chest for healing. I myself experienced prolonged outbursts of crying during those gatherings, regardless of how close or how far Baba was passing by. It was crying without hysteria, as if all the love in my heart were melting inside me, streaming quietly in tears. I had never known such blessing in my life.

After walking among the crowd, Baba would take a seat under the gazebo and lead us in the singing of bhajans (spiritual songs). Sometimes there was also an added ritual of lighting a fire in a vessel, or placing flowers on an altar, to end the one-hour or so of "darshan" (the blessing of being in the presence of a holy one). Baba would then return to his quarters, stopping on the way to invite small groups of visitors to a private audience, as was the case one morning when a delegation of about twenty women from Argentina, sitting close to me, had the privilege of receiving such an invitation from Baba himself. I would have loved to have gone to an audience, too, but I didn't dare to ask him, I just sat there transfixed by his presence.

The holy ash appearing from Baba's hands is a miracle the crowds around him have been witnessing for decades, and it happens every day. Once a year, as part of a religious ceremony attended by tens of thousands of people, hundreds of pounds of these ashes flow from an upside down empty jug, with a wave of the Master's hand; this incredible feat has baffled laymen and scientists alike. Baba also materializes other gifts in front of followers and skeptics, which range from watches, rosaries, rings and precious stones to fruit, candy, nectar, etc. When asked where those objects come from, Baba answers, "From the Sai stores." These miracles have been happening since Baba was four years old, when he started materializing sweets for his playmates.

On our two-week visit to Baba's ashrams in January-February 1983, I saw him produce ashes from the tip of his fingers into the extended hands of many people, several times. And once, when someone brought him a tray with a few pieces of wrapped candy, Baba started throwing them by the handful to students sitting along the way. In a few minutes, from the few pieces came hundreds of candies, to the delight of those who saw it. Somehow this reminded me of Jesus' feat of the fishes and the loaves. Baba loves to do these things for his devotees; he calls it his "calling card."

Born in Puttaparthi (Andhra Pradesh province, India) November 23, 1926, at age thirteen, young Sathya renamed himself Sai Baba and left home to teach a small group of followers. Now his devotees are counted in the millions and come from every religion and every corner of the world. He is considered by many to be an avatar[13]. His life of purity and service, his love and miracles, his teachings and example are clearly the traits of a superior being. As I said earlier, to me Baba is one of the holiest people walking this earth today, and I love him greatly.

Besides being a World Teacher, the adult life of Sathya Sai Baba has been dedicated to the education of his fellow Indians. More than forty colleges and universities founded and maintained by the Sathya Sai Baba Foundation, as well as many primary and high schools under the same organization, impart top quality education to a large number of young Indians. Modern hospitals and medical dispensaries for the poor are also part of Baba's concern for his people. The amazing thing about this huge endeavor is that a visitor to Baba's ashrams is never asked to contribute even a penny to his charities. Where the money comes from nobody really knows, except maybe those closest to him.

A few years ago we heard an interesting little story about Baba's money secrets: They say that two Indian officials had come to see Baba inquiring about the source of his income. "Oh, you want to know where the money comes from?" "It comes from above, like this." Rupees in all denominations started raining from the sky above the courtyard. The astonished investigators left in a hurry. Who knows!

While in India, I was the grateful recipient of one of Baba's miracles. Like many tourists, I came down with stomach trouble after eating some sweet curds we had

---

[13] *In Hinduism, a god's coming to earth in bodily form. (Webster's New World Dictionary).*

bought at a store one evening. Antacid did not help, and I spent a dreadful night throwing up and running to the bathroom. The headache and stomachache were almost unbearable the next morning; I was crying and sweating from pain. As soon as the shops opened, my husband left for the drugstore to find some appropriate medicine from the pharmacist. In the meantime I prayed and cried. Then I noticed on the night stand next to me a packet of vibuthi we had gotten at the ashram. Having seen people eat these ashes for healing purposes, I took the packet in my hands and mentally said, "Baba, I really need your help." Then I took a pinch of the ash and put it in my mouth, swallowing it with a sip of bottled water. The instant I swallowed the ashes the pain was gone, without a trace. It happened in a second; I was so very grateful. My husband came back with some medicines a few minutes later, but as he came to my bed I said to him, holding a finger to my lips: "Shhhhh, I am fine, I don't need anything else, I've been healed."

For almost fifteen years now, we have had a small jar (one-cup size) with the vibuthi we brought from India. We have taken it for healing, many times; we have put it on our hands and foreheads in the sign of the cross; I have rubbed ashes on my chest during asthma attacks, and we have also given away little packets of it to more than twenty people all these years, yet we have never run out of it. This phenomenon is not unusual among Baba's devotees. By his grace the ashes replenish themselves, and, in some cases, ash grows from pictures of Baba hanging in homes of devotees around the world. Another unusual thing is that the pleasant fragrance of the ashes has stayed fresh all these years.

## Chapter 12

# The Gift of Fragrances

I am not sure when I first noticed around me the three individual fragrances of roses, jasmine and sandalwood that I sometimes perceive, but I remember that one day in 1979, while driving on a highway in San Antonio, someone entering from an access road cut in front of me from the right, so close that I had to swerve towards the middle lane, momentarily, giving me quite a scare and leaving my heart pounding very fast. Within seconds I regained control and got back in the right lane. Then I noticed that a strong smell of roses filled the car, while at the same time I felt a sensation of calmness and safety taking hold of me, quite in contrast to the panicky moments I had just had. I felt a supernatural power was at work here, and I gratefully acknowledged it. I said, "thank you God, I am not alone."

The scent of roses has reappeared again at times of intense fright or worry, twice again while driving that same car, a Plymouth Horizon, which we had bought brand new and was never the same after we left it in storage for two years in San Antonio while we were in Saudi Arabia. The brakes alone gave me more than one good scare and so did the radiator, when it burst in the parking lot of the University of Texas in the Spring of 1986. On another occasion, when I brought the car to a garage near our house, after a long drive from school, knowing that something was wrong with it, the mechanic at the garage scratched his head after finding out the severity of the damage and couldn't figure out how I had driven the car with a crucial part missing. There was no doubt in my mind the angels were looking after me, and I was moved and grateful. The car was not fixed right even after changing mechanics, and we just about gave up on it. Not long after that I had my second near-death experience and God's helpers, once again, not only took care of me but offered to fix my car and did a good job at it. The chapter about my second near-death experience expands a bit more on this nice little miracle.

The jasmine fragrance can appear any time, for no apparent reason. It has happened while walking to the bus stop, while in class, in the kitchen, around the family, in the produce section of the supermarket; it can come absolutely anywhere. So does the sandalwood aroma. I ask people around me, if there are any, if anybody can smell the fragrance, but nobody else has ever noticed it. I also look around for flowerbeds or any possible source for the scents, but have never come up with any satisfactory explanation. I tend to associate the jasmine and the sandalwood scents with Sai Baba, and always thank God and Baba for those exquisite perfumes. The last time I smelled sandalwood was about a year ago when I said to myself, "Hum, it has been a while since I have smelled sandalwood." Within seconds a wonderful scent of sandalwood enveloped me.

Correction: On Monday April 28, 1997, I smelled sandalwood again, around a statue of Saint Rose placed in a corner of the main lobby at Santa Rosa Hospital Northwest, in San Antonio. I had gone there with my husband to sign a release form for some medical records, to take to my present doctor. On my way out I felt the familiar scent of sandalwood and immediately sniffed around the two big paintings on the wall and the statue of Saint Rose placed on a pedestal. The aroma was stronger around the statue. As I was leaving the lobby I decided to go back, twenty feet or so to the statue, for another sniff. The perfume was gone. I just smiled to myself and said thank you, God. Three days later I returned for the papers, and, on my way in and out of the lobby, I tested the spot for any perfume, again. None was sensed.

## Chapter 13

# Death's Own Perfume

There is one particular perfume that has been with me since my childhood. It is one I sense quite often, more often than the others, and again, it can happen anywhere. It is made of a mixture of flowers, and from an early age, as early as five, I have associated this scent with death. It scared my mother many times to hear me say, "I smell death." What did I know about death? The strange thing is, a few times we heard afterwards that somebody my family knew, had died or was gravely sick.

It got more disturbing when by the age of seven I was smelling this flowery perfume just about everywhere, in the streets, in church, or passing by the town's cemetery, which we had to pass, on the way to my father's small farm near the town. We would go to the farm about once a week to gather fresh vegetables and fruit for the family table, or to take lunch to my father and a helper or two at planting and harvest times; a walk of about thirty minutes with my six-year-old brother would often turn into a much longer trip when we stopped to catch minnows at the stream half way down the road. Smelling flowers around the cemetery would not have been unusual, but nobody else smelled them when I did, and, besides, paper flowers, which on a closer look we would find more often than natural ones, have no fragrance.

The smell of death was a premonition of things to come. In April 1948 civil war exploded in Colombia, after the assassination of a popular political leader, and the region where my family lived was attacked that same year with bloody results. I give a more complete account of this period of my life in the chapter entitled "Long Relationship with Death."

In my adult life, sometimes, the sensing of this perfume has coincided with deaths in the family, hundreds and even thousands of miles away, as when I was living in Indonesia in 1990 and two aunts passed away in Colombia, within a few months of each other. What I have learned to do is not to worry about it, but just ask God to help whoever is dying or is about to die, and is trying to let me know, to have an easy and loving transition. I even smelled this perfume not too long ago, twice, around an elderly lady, a friend of mine who has been seriously ill. Fortunately, she is still hanging on and back on her feet, to the delight of many of us who love her.

Not long ago (mid 1997) at a supermarket in San Antonio, as I passed by a bin of flowers near the cashier's desk, I discovered one component of this unusual perfume I associate with death. The fragrance emanating from some giant white chrysanthemums in the bin was like one of the scents in that special mixture of flowers I have known so long; to me this was an exciting discovery. Right after this happened I related the strange phenomenon of the perfumes I smell, to a lady doctor, a friend of many years, whose interests are wide and varied. She commented casually that chrysanthemums, to her, meant "farewell." That was very interesting to hear, because, to me, there is an undeniable sense of farewell in that perfume of death.

# Chapter 14

# Second NDE: A Promise of Music

On July 31, 1986 I was taken by ambulance from my home in San Antonio, to the nearest hospital, which happens to be Wilford Hall, the Air Force hospital at Lackland AFB, in the agony of a life-threatening asthma attack. I had done all I knew at home, such as treatments with the nebulizer and two injections of the emergency drug Terbutaline, without getting any relief. On the contrary I was fighting for my breath with every muscle of my body, sweating profusely from the great effort to get some air, unable to talk, with my sight getting blurrier by the minute. Riding in the ambulance, under an oxygen mask, I was in and out of darkness still suffering extreme oxygen deprivation because my lungs just couldn't open up enough to allow in much air. The ride to the hospital takes about 10 minutes, but that was too long for the condition I was in. I prayed and wondered if I would make it to the hospital alive. I did, barely.

As the emergency room people were connecting me to the oxygen, monitors and IVs, I suddenly felt sucked up by a tremendous force and started traveling at an incredible speed through a tunnel of black whirling light. I seemed to be in several places at the same time. One me was in the body, struggling for breath; another me was minding this "vehicle," fully aware of its crushing force and lightening speed; and a third me, detached and peaceful, observing all these happenings. As I entered into the brilliant white light at the other end of this upward-curving tunnel, I felt my heart slowing down to a stop, while at the same time seeing the nurses and doctor act very panicky, one of them saying, "Oh, no!"

Of what they did to my body after that, I did not become aware, nor did I care anymore. I was enraptured in God's love and joy, basking in His Light, and that was the only thing that mattered. In the light, a figure in white, including his hair, whom I took to be a master musician of old, whom I love, came forth and said to me: "When the time comes, we will have song and dance for you here." Then he embraced me gently and whispered, "friend," and walked away. The next thing I knew, I was back in my tired body, to the relief of the medical people in the emergency room. From then on my recovery, as it had been after my first NDE in 1982, was steady and smooth, leaving me in a blissful state of mind. Two days later I was transferred to Santa Rosa Catholic Hospital to continue treatment there for five more days.

The young Polish priest who brought me communion at Santa Rosa Hospital daily, stayed a while two or three times to say some comforting words to me. He was surprised to find me so upbeat and delighted to be in the hospital; I told him I was just glad to be back in the business of living, and related to him my very recent near-death experience and also my first one, four years earlier. He listened attentively, obviously moved, and commented once that while I was talking my countenance had become luminous. All I could answer him was, "such is the love of God." His eyes got teary; he held my hands and asked me to pray for him, then left.

This second NDE, like the first one, brought me some special gifts. My lungs felt wonderfully clean and perfect; I could breath as well as when I was fifteen; it was as if I had been given a brand-new pair of lungs. God's spirit healers also came, unexpectedly to me, to offer their help. While resting at home one day, not long after being discharged from the hospital, I heard a voice in my mind, asking if I wanted some healing. It was not a pleasant voice. Once, on television (the Johnny Carson show), I had seen an interview with the writer Truman Capote; the whimsical voice I had just heard reminded me of his voice. I blessed him and said I would be grateful to receive God's healing. Then, following his instructions, I relaxed, lay on my side, and mentally followed some kind of massage along my back and legs. At one point, I heard more than one voice and asked mentally who else was there. One male voice answered, "the healer Rose, is here; she is very knowledgeable." She greeted me saying, "Love, you are gonna need a lot of help with your legs," and then: "Child, we're here to serve you." The female voice had nuances of American Black speech.

It was true. My chest was fine, but the muscles in my legs were extremely week, and it was hard for me to walk. The healers suggested that I check my potassium and all the vital minerals. When I went to the doctor for a follow-up visit one week after my release from the hospital, I complained about the weakness in my legs and asked the doctor if it could be lack of potassium. He said it could well be because of the steroids I had received in the hospital and the maintenance dosage I was taking regularly. A test showed all my electrolytes to be low, with the potassium count dangerously low. I was put on a high potassium supplement. What a very useful lesson from my watchful healers.

After a few times of holding mental conversations with Rose and enjoying her massages, I asked if I could see her. The answer was, "Yes, get ready." I sat up in my bed, breathing slowly and evenly, with my eyes closed, without any tension in my body. In just a little while I had the lovely vision of a big, bosomy black woman with a jolly face; she looked to me like the mother of the whole world, kind and generous. From then on I would call her, affectionately, Mamma Rose. A few years later after encountering other wonderful angels and spirit healers, Mamma Rose has shown up with them several times, and her healing is always welcome. In the chapter "Healers in Disguise," I have a detailed account of those encounters.

In one of our healing sessions, the healers asked me if I wanted my car healed. I said to them that would be lovely. My car was in very bad shape indeed. It was the Plymouth Horizon I talked about in the chapter "The Gift of Fragrances." Mechanics had worked on it several times, but it was still very unreliable. On one occasion, when I took the car back to the garage (belonging to a big national chain of stores), where they had supposedly fixed everything after a second scare with failing brakes, the mechanic who took the car for a test drive around the neighborhood, had himself a scare of his own. We invested some more money on repairs, but the car just didn't feel right.

After a little while the healers told me the car was fixed, and they advised me to drive it to the Bible study meeting I was going to have the same Monday morning. I wasn't very sure I wanted to drive that far, and told them I would drive it to the supermarket first, a short distance from my house. Their answer was "As you like!" The healers had done a fine job with the car, and from then on it worked well for my husband and me (the only drivers at our home) until June of 1987 when we sold it to help pay for a vacation in Colombia for me and our two sons that summer.

Busy with the concerns of this world, my family, my friends, housekeeping, my studies, etc., I lost contact with the healers, since I was not taking enough time to relax, pray and meditate. My chest slowly returned to its previous wheezy and congested state; I could not hold on to my miracle; the circuit had been interrupted; my subconscious or some level of my mind had not completely accepted the healing; something in me, that I didn't understand, was blocking the gift of health.

## Chapter 15

# Third NDE: The Joy of Surrender, Bargaining with God.

Sunday February 1, 1987, I landed in the emergency room of St. Rose Hospital again, with a severe asthma attack. They had almost gotten used to seeing me, at least twice a year, in their emergency room and intensive care unit. Someone would recognize me and say, with a touch of compassion, "Oh, it's you again. We are so sorry."

This time their timely intervention and two days in intensive care put me on a clear way to recovery, or so we thought. I was transferred to a semi-private room to continue treatment until my lungs cleared up satisfactorily. But my infected and congested sinuses made breathing through my nose rough going. Although I was connected to an oxygen mask twenty-four hours a day, constant mouth breathing was tiring and made eating difficult, not being able to breath well through my nose. My doctor advised that I take a sinus decongestant, and prescribed one. For two days I refused to take that medicine, because I vaguely remembered that about two years earlier the same drug had given me a bad reaction. That was the reason I gave the doctor for my refusal to take it when he came again on his daily rounds, but he assured me there wasn't anything harmful for me in that decongestant. On Saturday February 7th, I was so sick and tired of having a stopped up nose, that, after lunch, I asked the nurses for the tablet.

Within two hours of taking the medicine, my blood pressure went up to a dangerously high level, triggering the alarm of the monitoring equipment connected to me. An unbearable headache also accompanied the rising blood pressure. I was fighting for my life, and my doctor could not be located that Saturday afternoon.

At the height of the agony, my husband arrived for his daily visit, only to see me again on the brink of death. While the nurses tried some emergency measures, I was giving up, resigned to taking the final step. I said to myself, "my life doesn't depend on any machine or drugs anymore, it is in the hands of God." "Thy will be done." Suddenly, I saw a great explosion take place within me, leaving a lot of ashes and debris scattered around, and one wall standing. Everything was ablaze, but there was no sign of me. Next I saw my body reclined in the hospital bed, still alive, but barely, a great big transparent bubble slowly lifting from my head. Looking at my body I thought: "I am still alive, I am whole." From every place of my being, including the bubble and the scattered ashes, I asked God to spare my life once more. And He did. From that moment on breathing became easier and more relaxed, and the headache and the high blood pressure descended, almost in a vertical way, like looking at a thermometer coming down. I knew all was well. The extreme nose and head congestion had cleared up as if by magic.

The same deep joy and gratitude I had experienced after my two prior NDEs in 1982 and 1986, returned anew, to the surprise of those attendants who had witnessed this latest close call.

Prayer, too, had been a big part of the miracle. Right after my emergency hospitalization, February 1st., my husband had called our church (St. Rose of Lima) and some Baptist friends to ask for prayers; I am sure every bit helped.

Our Baptist friends (husband and wife) came to visit me the next day, Sunday the 8th. I was eating lunch with gusto when they arrived, and they were pleased to find me in excellent spirits and well into recovery. The conversation turned later to my relating the extraordinary occurrence of the day before. When they heard my story, their joy turned into disbelief and fear in front of my eyes. Without saying it directly, they implied that the whole event had been a trick of the devil, always looking for an opportunity to gain points with us humans, when they pointed out to me that the "deceiver" was always around. They offered to pray some more and even invited me and my family to go to a weekly prayer group at their home.

These were good people, and we liked them well, but beliefs founded on fear and stiff concepts are a sad thing to see. I know in my heart that when you call on God for help, being a loving father/mother to all, He will not fail you. As the Bible says, just as your human father will not give you a stone when you ask for bread, neither will your heavenly father. We did go to their prayer meetings a number of times. Prayer is imbued with good will, and none of it is lost, yours or mine.

On the 12th of February I was released from the hospital. Those twelve days had done a lot of good to my body and spirit. I came home, and remained, for the following three weeks, in an altered state of consciousness that manifested itself in different ways. I felt at peace with everything, and everything was at peace with me; I could see clearly (clairvoyantly) and understood that everything and everyone in the world had a reason for being, with a purpose and a goodness about them; I could not get worried or angry at anything. Something else in my body had been affected in a strange way: my blood pressure would not register anything at all, on a machine at the supermarket, even though the people going before and after me were getting their readings without any problem. Out of curiosity we tried the same machine several times, three days apart, with the same odd results; it didn't bother me, and I didn't think anybody else should be too concerned. On the other hand, the radio at home was acting weird, turning itself on if I came close to it.

Once again that wonderful blessed state my NDE had triggered started to wear out; I drifted back, little by little, into the denser affairs of life in the body, "the ritual of the habitual," as they say. Unfortunately for me, that meant also being sick most of the time.

In July (1987) the boys and I went to Colombia on a six-week vacation, and we had a wonderful visit with my family. We had not seen most of my relatives in eleven years, although my mother, and a sister and her husband, had had a short visit with us in the States once during those long years. We crisscrossed more than half of my country's rich and contrasting geography, getting a taste of climates and scenery ranging from the very warm lowlands at sea level, to passing near the perennial snow-capped peaks and volcanoes of the Andes, at altitudes of 12,000 feet and above, with very cold temperatures, and then to the balmy Caribbean coast. All that pleasure was necessary in order to visit my mother and six of my seven brothers and sisters, residing in different parts of the country. My young boys (aged 13 and 18 then), were thrilled to travel by Land Rover up and down the high Andean mountains with their uncle Humberto. There were scary moments traveling in the mountains, though. At the higher altitudes those winding roads were reduced to just two lanes of steady traffic, often going at speeds faster than it was prudent to drive in that kind of terrain. Drops hundreds of feet deep were visible from our windows, and the vehicle felt too close to the edge of the road at times, and in some spots there were no guard rails at all; it was nerve racking at best. Several accidents along the road reminded us of how dangerous traveling in the mountains can be. The ever present danger of guerrilla warfare was also in our minds and not without reason. At one point, a bridge on the route we were traveling, parallel to the one we crossed, had been blown up by guerrillas the night before and was still smoking. Colombian army personnel were all around.

There were eighteen cousins my sons did not remember or had not met before. Meeting them was very exciting and a challenge for my boys at the same time, since their Spanish language skills were not the best. They managed to communicate and have a good time as well. Under the expert instruction of their Colombian cousins, my two shy gringos learned to dance to the Latin beats in no time at all.

A month and a half was really too short for the three of us to catch up with eleven years away from my family. Just when my sons were getting used to the language and the changes in culture, we had to come back to the United States to prepare to go back to school at the end of August. I was attending the University of Texas in San Antonio (UTSA), with at least two more years to go before graduation (as an undergraduate). Anyway, I was grateful for the family reunion and the beneficial effect the change in environment had had on my allergies and asthma.

# Chapter 16

# Out-of-body Experiences

I am a dreamer and a flyer (I fly in my dreams), but I have never had any interest in learning about out-of-body or astral traveling, nor do I have any idea of what causes it. Nevertheless, it has happened to me spontaneously, many times.

Flying on your own power is one of the most enjoyable sensations you can have; it is freedom at its best. I think I fly most of the time for rest and for the pleasure of my soul. How else can I explain the playful and unconcerned manner in which I find myself flying in my dreams. I go up vertically, horizontally, sitting cross-legged, and even feet first. I fly through walls and windows and over trees, cliffs and mountains, in a variety of patterns and positions. Sometimes I just leap and dance in the air for the joy of it.

For years, in my dreams, I have visited Falan, the small town in the Andes Mountains of Colombia where I was born (March 24, 1941.) I have hovered over its streets, paths and roads and flown around its mountains and streams. At times I have seen the living and the dead together, around the main plaza. Consciously I am not aware of any reason or attachment that would pull me to the town I left for good at age fifteen, yet I keep going back in my dreams, once or twice a year, to that place, watching it from above but not actually landing. A few times in those dreams I had trouble getting caught on lines while flying; it was annoying and confusing to find those kinds of obstacles when you least expected them.

In the summer of 1994, I went to Colombia on a vacation, and also with the purpose of bringing my mother to the United States to live with us for a while. I had the opportunity to travel to my hometown of Falan, in the Department of Tolima, after not having been there for twenty-eight years; my mother and a niece accompanied me. As we wound our way up the mountains (the town is at an altitude of about five thousand feet), I noticed that not far from the road, along the way, there were huge towers, holding high tension, electric transmission lines to the town and beyond. The puzzle was solved. Those were the lines I had been getting tangled up with in my dreams. Those towers didn't exist in my youth, when the town was self-sufficient in getting its electric power from a small hydro-electric plant on one of the rivers. They must have outgrown their power capacity. As to the reasons for my astral traveling to that location, after seeing the splendid scenery and views around the town, I came to the conclusion that what kept me coming back again and again in my dreams had to be the beauty of the region.

There is, however, a more serious aspect to flying, as in the case of hovering over your body during the near-death experience, bi-location, and astral traveling to other realms of the universe for the purpose of knowledge and enlightenment. I have been aware of those occasions, too. During my second NDE, for example, I was conscious of being in three places at the same time.

When eager souls are ready for knowledge, God provides the means and the teachers, be it in earthly classrooms or heavenly ones. In my flying dreams I have seen souls coming and going to "school" and remember several times paying attention to see if I could recognize any of my daylight friends among them. I have seen a couple of them.

In 1985 I had a very powerful out-of-body experience. I was at home by myself one morning; the children were at school and my husband at work. I had been having a rough time with asthma and the medicines themselves were making me sick. Feeling rather discouraged, I sat in bed praying and crying silently, after taking a treatment with the nebulizer. Suddenly, I found myself in a vast lake, in a state of complete calmness. I felt the cool and clear waters and the breeze from above, all at once. Then I realized I was the water, the breeze, the sky, and everything in sight – all-inclusive, in perfect agreement. I thought it would be wonderful to stay there, but then I thought, "Cliff (my husband) won't know what happened." Looking from somewhere away, I observed my body still sitting in bed and thought: "There is poor Gloria, and she is not breathing." Unperturbed, I came back into my body and tried to help myself to breathe by opening my mouth. I don't know how long I was away, but my body was icy cold. Conscious deep breathing and a couple of blankets wrapped around me brought me back to daily life.

On several occasions, during meditation, I have caught myself not breathing or just as the breath was stopping, and have calmly come back to reassume the respiratory functions.

## Chapter 17

# The Anointing of the Sick

Caring for asthma is never routine, or easy, at least in my case. Unpredictable reactions to medicines, food and the environment, most of which have proved very evasive to testing and treatment over the years, has kept me walking the tight rope of my life gingerly, but determined to go on, nonetheless.

In the 80s, in between daily asthma attacks and several life-threatening crises, including three NDEs, I tried to fit in my household chores, raising two children, church activities, studies at the university, traveling, and looking for a cure, the best I could. I love studying and the arts, and God gave me a good mind and enthusiasm to apply myself to anything I like, but there is no denying that chronic illness since 1970, has been a heavy burden for me to carry.

At the end of 1988, I was very sick again with bronchitis, on top of daily respiratory troubles. I asked my husband to call the priest at Saint Rose of Lima church, and ask him if he could bring me the anointing of the sick. Father Kevin agreed to come that same Friday evening, and gave my husband some instructions as to what to prepare. My husband placed a small table by my bed, covered it with a folded tablecloth and set a Bible on it; then he briefed our sons on the meaning of the sacrament and on what to do in response to the priest's prayers and readings. With everything set for the rites, we waited, and waited for the priest, but by ten at night, or later, he still had not showed up or called.

That night I had a wonderful dream. *I was in an empty church of round shape, with glistening walls, the color of honey. The priest, in white, signaled me to come to the altar. As I approached the altar, I noticed his beautiful, kind eyes. He took in his hands a golden round dish with a cover, and opened it, to give me communion. But there were no wafers in the dish; instead there was a square cross, with ends in the shape of three-pointed leaves, like "fleurs de lis," and in the center of the cross a shiny, red stone, like a ruby. The priest took out the cross, and anointed me with it on my forehead and on the palms of my hands. Feeling faint, I told the priest so. He answered, "don't worry; we'll take care of you." Next, I was lying on the ground next to the altar, resting peacefully.* End of the dream.

What an extraordinary anointing. I was amazed and grateful at God's grace, and how He loves us and tends to our needs and desires. Upon waking up on Saturday morning, I felt much better, too.

On Sunday I was able to go to mass. After the mass ended, as the priest was coming out to greet the parishioners, he saw me as he passed by, and stopped to say he had just remembered we had called him on Friday for the sacrament of the sick. He was really embarrassed about having forgotten the appointment. I told him: "Don't worry father, I got it better. I received a wonderful anointing from above." I related to him my dream, quickly. He didn't know what to say.

Something comforting is always at hand when I reach in surrender or even in desperation or anger for God's help. Many times I have asked Mother God (Yes, God is mother too), "I am tired, I am hurting, take me in your arms, please Divine Mother" and then let go, close my eyes and feel like a baby in its mother's lap. How soothing those moments have been to me when nothing else seemed to help. Many good cries and prayer have also been useful. Such was the case when I had the spontaneous out-of-body experience I described in the preceding chapter. Dreams of great beauty and enjoyment have come to me following very painful and life-threatening crises, and, of course, the welcome help of the angels and healers has been essential to my survival. Even my deceased father has shown up to acknowledge his love and concern for me. One night when I had struggled very hard with a severe asthma attack for hours and finally had fallen half asleep in the early morning hours, I saw my father standing at the feet of my bed, dressed in white, holding a candle in his hands and smiling. I tried to say, "Papa is here" and push my husband with my elbow, but I couldn't move. When I was able to sit up, my father was gone. I was very moved by his loving appearance.

## Chapter 18

# A Welcomed Assignment

In-country assignments with the Defense Language Institute are very rare, but in 1989 the Saudi Arabian Navy had sent a group of its navy personnel for training at the Pensacola Naval Air Station, and DLI was asked to send two English instructors to NAS Pensacola. My husband quickly volunteered for one of the two positions. We were very familiar with the area, since my husband had spent part of his youth in Pensacola, graduating from high school there, and we had, over the years, traveled there once or twice a year to visit his parents.

We welcomed the opportunity to go to Florida, since my father-in-law was living in a nursing home in Pensacola, suffering from advanced amiotrophic lateral sclerosis (Lou Gehrig's disease). At that time grandpa's speech and movement were already greatly impaired, but his mind was sharp, and his good sense of humor undiminished.

We loved every moment of our stay in Pensacola, and the privilege of giving grandpa lots of love and affection, especially since he was lonely after the death of his wife of 57 years (my mother-in-law), a little over a year earlier. Grandpa's other two children lived in Michigan and Iowa and could not be with him more than a few weeks a year. With our two sons we visited him once or twice a week in the nursing home and sometimes brought with us our beagle "Spicy" for him to pet. Beagles were one of his favorite breeds of dogs. As a child on his family farm in southern

Indiana, my father-in-law had had beagles around him. Even in his semi-paralyzed condition, grandpa laughed and relished the dog's display of affection for him.

Grandpa was loved by everyone at the nursing home and by everyone who ever knew him – a truly fair and lovable man. He had been a firefighter for more than 40 years, retiring as Fire Chief of Ellyson Field, a navy helicopter training facility in Pensacola. He died June 20, 1994 at age 89 in perfect use of his mind, to the point that he asked the nurses the morning of his death to please call his three children because he thought he was dying. We called him back to reassure him that there wasn't anything new or serious in his condition to think about dying, but he knew better. About three hours later his daughter in Detroit called to inform us her father had just died in Pensacola, very quietly at around noon.

Coincidentally, our noble beagle Spicy, the one grandpa had enjoyed so much when we lived near him, died unexpectedly at age 14, the 4th of February 1997, the day that Grandpa would have celebrated his birthday. Coincidence?

## Chapter 19

# Healers in Disguise

Pensacola has its charm and the whitest beaches I have ever seen, but my troubles from asthma, sinusitis and allergies became even more severe there than they had been in San Antonio; I was having at least one bad attack every day, and my doctors were at a loss for a medical solution.

On Saturday December 9, 1989, in the afternoon, I arrived by ambulance at Sacred Heart Hospital with a very severe asthma attack. After spending several hours in the emergency room and the ICU, under aggressive treatment and a respirator, once my condition became more stable, I was sent to a small private room (no semi-private rooms were available), with an IV line on each arm and a catheter in my bladder. My husband stayed with me until around midnight, when he was chased out of the hospital. He wanted to stay with me and maybe get a little sleep resting on the comfortable chair in my room, but he was not allowed to stay. These kinds of rules have never made any sense to me. Nothing brings more comfort and encouragement to a sick person than having a loved one nearby.

Exhausted from the long struggle for breath all day, I, too, wanted to sleep, but it wasn't easy with half a dozen gadgets attached to my body, most of them painful and restraining. On top of that my bed could not be made to go down from the center to the end, so I wasn't able to stretch my legs. The mechanism had gotten stuck, and neither the nurses nor my husband could figure out how to make it move. In that uncomfortable sitting position, with my knees bent high and a catheter hurting inside, the only sleep I got that night, on and off, was three hours at the most.

Around 5:55 a.m. Sunday I was sitting very still with my eyes closed, trying to get some more needed sleep, when suddenly the bed started going down (at the feet), and I could hear the motor's noise. I opened my eyes to see if the nurse was there, but there was nobody on either side of my bed. When the motor stopped, the side of my bed that had been stuck was lowered flat. A little past 6:00 a.m., a nurse came into my room to take my temperature and blood pressure, as they do every few hours. I told her about my bed moving by itself and she said: "Poltergeist with your bed, ah?"

Just after she left the room I heard a voice inside me say: "That was to get you started with your visualization exercises. And, do them not twice but three times a day."

I had been doing some visualization exercises for a few weeks already, as taught in the book "Healing Visualizations: Creating Health Through Imagery" by Gerald Epstein, M.D., which says you should bring and hold in your mind, very briefly, images of the healing you want, repeating the exercise two or more times every day. It had all started in a mysterious way. A book I had not requested arrived in the mail one day in October from a book club I belonged to. I wasn't pleased with the mistake and planned to return the book to the sender the next day. But something pushed me to open it, even though I knew I had to send it back in its original package and opening it meant I had to buy it. When I saw what kind of book it was, I was dumbfounded. I thought: "God, I needed this book, thank you God." So, those were the visualization exercises that inner voice and instructions referred to.

Doing the exercises took very little time, since each one lasts from only one to two minutes. Once I finished them and unable to sleep anymore, I began to think about breakfast. I had not eaten since noon Saturday and by Sunday morning I was really hungry.

Amidst my thoughts of food I heard a voice again, this time offering healing. I said, mentally, I would welcome it and would be very grateful to have it. I was directed to relax and follow with my mind the massage and healing I was going to receive. With my eyes closed, I "saw" three "people" wearing pale blue gowns, like those worn by patients in hospitals. They started massaging my lungs, my kidneys, my whole back and my chest. I asked them, "Why the blue gowns?" They said they could wear anything they wanted but, since I tended to associate blue with healing, they were wearing that color for me. I also asked them if they were good at this work, and one said they were considered very good healers. I could hear them joking and laughing as they worked, and I told them they didn't sound very serious to me. One of them responded: "What do you expect? We are clowns." "We used to heal with laughter, and we still do it that way here." Another one added: "And, we know you well; you are well known here; you are one of us." (I knew what they meant, and I will explain it later in the section entitled "More men in white.") I asked them to help me with the discomfort from the catheter. Somehow they did, and I felt a lot better. They told me the gadget would be removed in a little while, and it was; late that morning by doctor's order; one of the IVs was disconnected, also.

I commented about a song, from a musical, called "Send in the Clowns" that I had heard on television and told them I thought the words were a bit ridiculous for the beautiful melody the song had. "You won't think it is ridiculous anymore," one clown said. "In fact from now on, anytime you need us, just say 'Send in the clowns'; we'll be around; call us anytime." They advised me to do one specific visualization exercise more often, to help my lungs. I thanked them, embraced them and said good bye to them, mentally. The whole episode was most enjoyable. It had lasted in "real" time about one hour. (True to their promise, the clowns stayed around me for almost two years, helping me and my family with our daily affairs and producing, for all of us to enjoy, all kinds of little, and not so little, miracles.)

A nurse's aid came to give me a sponge bath, and a little later they brought me breakfast. Dr. Brown came towards noon and was impressed with the progress I had made but, still, wanted to keep me in the hospital for a whole week.

A stay of four days was all I allowed, convincing the doctor I would take good care of myself at home, and that I would just "supervise" the preparations for our moving back to Texas in two weeks. I continued to receive healing and direction from my spiritual friends almost daily.

One curious coincidence is that since childhood I have loved to draw or doodle clowns' faces on papers, notebooks, and even on fogged up windows. It just gives me pleasure to do that. Seeing these three clowns with my mind's eye was amusing to me but not a total surprise. Besides, I had been helped before, in times of need, by angels and healers from above when with all my heart I had asked "Beloved God, send your angels and your healers to help me, please." Relief or healing had not been long in forthcoming. Thus, I was somewhat used to unusual happenings. Prayer and gratitude have been an important part of my life since childhood, except for some fifteen years in my youth, when I had a rebellious spell with times of disbelief, and then again a renewed search for God.

Regardless of my troubles, we had enjoyed our year in Pensacola a lot and were very grateful to God for allowing us to be close to my father-in-law one whole year. It was time to move on, and this time it looked like it would be half way across the world.

## Chapter 20

# Miracles All the Way

Towards the end of our "tour" in Pensacola, my husband was offered a two-year assignment in Indonesia. Over the years we had heard many good things about Indonesia from instructors who had worked there, and in the past my husband had volunteered to go, without success. Now they were offering him the post and, with it, a temporary promotion for the duration of the assignment. We were very pleased with the offer and eager to go to the Far East. That meant we had to start overseas processing as soon as we returned to San Antonio, and again start sorting and dividing our household goods to leave the nonessentials in storage.

Christmas week 1989 was one of the coldest ever for the South of the United States. Temperatures stayed in the teens or low 20s for several days, a rare happening for the lower south. In Pensacola we were under a deep freeze for at least three days in a row. The little old house we had rented in Navy Point, near the base, only had a floor furnace in the center of the house, and it proved completely inadequate for the intense cold spell we were having. We bought two portable heaters, but even with those on, the house was still very cold. The first night of the freeze we left a trickle of water running in the tub, and what we found the next morning was a thick sheet of ice in the tub and no running water.

With the movers coming early on the 26th to pack and ship our household goods, I looked at the pile of at least two days' worth of dirty dishes, wishing there were a way to have them clean for the packers the next day. The kitchen was very cold, so I went to sit down by the furnace to warm up my feet and hands. A moment later I heard water running in the kitchen sink, full blast. I was so grateful, I cried. This became our only source of water for the next 24 hours. Nothing else had opened up but the one I had wished for.

Houses like that one, built on stilts, and poorly insulated, dating from the time of WW II were the hardest hit. There were many broken pipes in the neighborhood, including the houses on each side of ours. None of our pipes broke or suffered any damage.

The pattern of "help by the asking" or even by just thinking about it, became a regular occurrence in our house. I seemed to be plugged into a direct line of wonders since my encounter with the clowns in the hospital. I received guidance about every concern of ours, no matter how small. My health, the preparations for moving back to San Antonio, paper work, running the house, every task became easier and smoother with help from above. Even our big, old 78 Chrysler New Yorker performed well and gave us no trouble on our long trip back to Texas.

Once in San Antonio, we moved to a motel near Lackland AFB, since we were between assignments and our own house had been rented out and was occupied by tenants. We started processing for Indonesia immediately, but there were a few delays in getting all our visas ready. When they finally arrived, one of our sons' passports was missing. Monday, March 4, 1990 at noon, Lackland asked my husband to leave on the appointed day, early Wednesday morning, with one of our sons and to leave me behind with the younger boy until his missing passport and visa arrived. They thought it would be easier to change the departure date on two tickets than on all four. My clowns, however, assured me that the family would travel together. And true to their promise, by closing time Monday, the passport arrived at the overseas section of DLI (Defense Language Institute).

Another pressing problem was getting rid of the car. My husband was losing hope and thought we would have to take it to the dealer and sell it for peanuts. Again the clowns advised me not to worry and told me we were going to get a fair price and be very satisfied with the deal. The problem was we only had one day left to do it. A lady to whom we had offered the car some weeks earlier, called us Monday night and said she was interested but had to get the money through a bank and it would take some work. I was completely confident we had a buyer. Tuesday, just before noon, she called me to say she had the $2,000 and would be meeting us at the courthouse that afternoon. She had not seen the old Chrysler but found it a real bargain and looking very good for a car that age. We finished transferring the title just before the county office closed at five p.m., and everybody was quite satisfied. (When we visited these friends again in 1994, they told us they still had the car and had traveled in it as far as Canada and back).

So, with this last hurdle crossed, we took the bus back to the motel and walked with the children to a nearby restaurant to have our last meal in San Antonio before our departure for Indonesia, at six in the morning the next day (March 6, 1990), very much relieved and grateful that all was well.

# Chapter 21

# The Beauty of the Orient

After a stop in Tokyo and a day in Singapore, we arrived in Jakarta, the capital of Indonesia, located in the western part of the island of Java, the evening of March 9, 1990. My husband's new supervisor and another member of the English language training team, stationed in Jakarta, welcomed us at the airport. We saw little of the capital that night on our ride to the city, except for the first impressions at the airport, which I consider one of the most beautiful airports I have ever been through. We were taken to an American embassy guest house (an apartment, actually), and spent the following three days mostly at the embassy, where my husband had to get acquainted with the details of his new post in Yogyakarta, a city of about one million people, in Central Java. Among other things the three-day pause gave us a chance to recover from jet lag.

More than five million people lived in Jakarta at that time, and the city seemed busy as a beehive, and so was the whole island of Java, we were told. Of the total 180 million population of Indonesia at that time, 120 million people lived on Java alone, making it, by size, one of the most populated places on earth.

Two U.S. military officers accompanied us to Yogyakarta, one hour away from the capital by plane, where we were greeted by a group of Indonesian Air Force officials. And since my husband's new place of work was located at the other side of the airport, they drove us to see the facilities first. A nice little reception had been prepared for us at the base, with pastries, hors d'oeuvres, punch and tea. The Indonesian officials then showed us the room that was going to be my husband's office, telling us Pope John Paul II had been in that same office, at that same desk, just a few months earlier when he had visited Yogyakarta and gotten a short tour of the base – a nice anecdote. They also joked about the room being "holy."

It was a beautiful sunny morning in Yogya (as the people of Java call the ancient city of Yogyakarta.) The U.S. officers we had traveled with had also tipped us about the fact that Indonesians love to abbreviate every word they can.

Afterwards we drove to our new home, some 10 miles from the airport, in two Indonesian Air Force vehicles. On the way home the U.S. Air Force colonel riding with us in one of the cars, told me he personally had selected the house and signed the lease. He thought we would be pleased, but warned us the street leading to the house was in horrible shape. The surprise to him and to us was that when we got to it, the street was newly paved. The house, as he had anticipated, was very nice, with marble floors, a living room with arches and ceiling of beautifully carved wood and an elegant chandelier; three large bedrooms; two bathrooms; a large sitting room, and a garage. Besides, there were, in back, complete living quarters for a servant or two, plus the kitchen and a laundry room. The furniture the embassy had installed in our new home was plentiful and adequate, but it looked modest in the fancy little mansion. My delight was the front garden, carefully manicured, facing an ample, arched corridor, or porch, where one could sit to catch the breeze and relax.

To the north, a chain of high mountains overlooked the city. The highest of them was the perfectly pointed Mount Merapi, an active volcano that had been smoking continuously for many years already. It was a breathtaking sight. We could view the fuming top of Merapi from our house on cloudless days. To the south, less than an hour's drive away, was the Indian Ocean. The beaches, however, were not suitable for swimming, due to the constant roughness of the waves on that part of Java.

Thanks to an Indonesian Air Force officer, Capt. Sonny, chief English instructor at the Indonesian Air Force Academy where my husband worked as an advisor, I was able to find my away around Yogya. He showed us places to shop and the three different offices where we would have to pay our utilities.

Help from above and the guidance of the clowns were also present. It often came in the form of synchronicity and coincidences such as the opening of a supermarket a few blocks from our house, the electric company opening a branch within walking distance soon after, and finding a language academy within walking distance, where we could go for Indonesian language instruction. The language academy put me in contact with several foreign people who spoke English or Spanish, and some of them were right in the neighborhood. The paving of our street, I learned later from my friends in the neighborhood, was an isolated case since the rest of the streets were left unpaved as they had been for years. By the end of our two years in Yogya, those streets were still unpaved. To make things more puzzling, only about eight blocks of our street had been paved, leaving a long stretch farther away from our house undone. It seems that someone was making things easier for us.

There was no culture shock to speak of, at least for me. In fact, I would call my introduction to Indonesia love at first sight. The rest of the family adjusted to the culture relatively well, too. Of all my travels, I had felt these "welcome back" feelings only in two places before: India and Spain, but never as intense as in Java. I found myself weeping for joy several times while looking at people passing by, or contemplating the scenery of luscious vegetation and rice paddies everywhere around. I would say in a whisper, "Oh God, how I love this place..." Everyone and everything seemed so lovely in this city.

Another member of the team of five people from the Defense Language Institute my husband was part of, had arrived in Indonesia a few months ahead of us and was working as a language advisor at the military academy in Magelang, about two hours from Yogyakarta. George, an old friend of ours, had worked with my husband many years, at Lackland and in Saudi Arabia. He had already made himself at home in Magelang, had learned some Indonesian, and was acquainted with most of Central Java, including Yogya. On several weekends he graciously showed us around some restaurants and places of interest, both in his town and in ours, and put us in contact with a Buddhist center in the neighboring town of Solo. I visited the center several times for classes and meditation. The other three members of the DLI team were working farther away at a naval base in Surabaya on the eastern side of Java and in the capital of Jakarta in the west, and we didn't see them that often.

One of the most interesting places George took us to see, a few weeks after our arrival, was Borobudur, an ancient Buddhist temple, and the biggest Buddhist monument in the world, located between Yogya and Magelang. Dating from the eighth and ninth centuries, it is built on an artificial hill, in the shape of a square with five levels of terraces followed by three circular levels to the top. It is a place of pilgrimage and beauty, where pilgrims re-enact the Buddhist journey of enlightenment by circling the terraces and gradually ascending to the higher levels until they reach the top, which represents nirvana or ultimate truth. Thousands of bas-relief carvings on the walls of the first terraces depict the life of the Buddha. There are a total of 504 statues of "the enlightened one" throughout the temple, including 72 of them under giant bell-shaped stupas[14] on the three higher circles of the temple. Every year, on May 8, Buddhists from all over the world converge at Borobudur to celebrate the birth of Gautama Buddha, the master who was born in India 535 years before the birth of Jesus Christ.

Borobudur lay buried for almost a thousand years under the ashes from an eruption of Mount Merapi, until 1814 when it was rediscovered by Thomas Raffles, then Governor of Java. Reconstruction was started at the beginning of this century, but real progress was not made until the temple was recognized as a "world heritage monument" and the United Nations pledged its support to rebuild it in 1973. Ten years later this grandiose monument was opened to the public. I had the privilege of visiting this marvelous temple twice.

Although just about everything we found in Yogya was to our liking, we did have one unpleasant situation to deal with. There was a couple living in the servants' quarters, hired to look after the house before we moved in. The man had been employed by the owner of the house, an Indonesian Air Force colonel, and according to custom, we were supposed to keep him and pay his salary from the moment we moved in. His duties were as a watchman at night and as gardener a few hours a week. Having a watchman, we were told, was a "must" for foreigners living in Java, and for rich Indonesians as well. I, however, was very uncomfortable with the arrangement and did not like having two people around I couldn't communicate with. On top of that, the man for some reason scared me. He had a strange look in his eyes that gave me a very uneasy feeling. He was ugly looking by nature, but physical ugliness I don't mind; it was his eyes that bothered me. The woman was pleasant and smiled a lot, but I didn't know what her duties were or what she was there for at all. As far I was concerned, I didn't need any help in running the house, except maybe for cleaning the floors, because the exertion made my chest tight and started me coughing for hours. She stayed a lot in their room, or out of the house.

One day the woman looked very sick and pale. Gesturing, I asked her what was wrong. She gestured back by putting her arms around and away from her stomach to mean pregnancy and then gestured that the baby had come out, like in a miscarriage. The man was sleeping in a long chair in the garage and we woke him up. I told him to take her to the hospital, and he did. ("Rumah sakit," hospital in the Indonesian language, was one of the first words I had learned, since we asthmatics never know when we will end up in an emergency room.) The next day they came back, the woman looking a little better.

---

[14] *A dome enclosing an effigy of Buddha.*

Shortly after that incident, with the help of an American lady, a long-time resident of Yogya, doing the translation for me, I learned that the woman living in my house had four more children and that her mother was taking care of them, the watchman being the father of one of them. I was advised not to get sucked into these kinds of problems and to get rid of these two people. They had been with us two months. We offered the man a bonus equivalent to two extra months of salary, and he was eager to take it and leave.

We decided not to hire a watchman anymore and never afterwards saw the need for one either, but the embassy wasn't very happy with our decision, in part because they felt responsible for our safety in Indonesia, and partly because having a watchman was expected of foreigners. My husband was the only official U.S. government employee in Yogya, as far as we knew, but being an English language advisor is hardly a position of any social or political consequence; so we were not any less or more visible than the other foreigners in town. We did hire a woman to come daily to help with the household chores and a gardener one day every two weeks, but no live-in help. These two people were well-recommended, very likable and good workers.

In July 1990, just four months after being in Yogyakarta, I had my first severe asthma attack there that required hospitalization. It happened while my husband was out of town. He had gone to Jakarta to take care of our banking needs at the U.S. embassy. Since there were no banks in Yogya that would accept our personal checks without the international transaction taking several weeks, plus a substantial commission, we were allowed to travel to the capital periodically to change, each time, enough dollars into rupias (the Indonesian monetary unit) to last us about two months. Our two boys (then 16 and 21 years old) were with me at the time, and seeing the seriousness of the attack, called a neighbor, an American missionary, for help. Mr. Humble took me to the emergency room of the nearest hospital, an ER with very little in the way of fancy equipment, but provided with oxygen and the drugs needed to treat life-threatening asthma. After the worse of the attack was over, I was put in a small room, where my medical needs would be tended. When Mr. Humble and his wife and my younger son came to visit me in the afternoon, I learned that my husband had been contacted in Jakarta and that he would be taking the first available flight back home. He arrived early the next morning since he had not been able to get on any flight from Jakarta the day before.

Concerned about my personal comfort, the Humbles had made arrangements for my transfer to a bigger nearby hospital. They thought I would be able to rest much better in an air-conditioned room. Most of the rooms in the hospital I was in didn't have air conditioning; the few that had it were all taken, and it looked doubtful they would have an air-conditioned room available any time soon.

The VIP room (that's what it was called) I was taken to, at the more modern Bethesda Hospital, was a spacious, air-conditioned room, with an extra bed for company and plenty of sitting room for family and friends to visit with the patient; the bathroom had a separate shower and a tub to choose from. The only other place where I had enjoyed a hospital room that nice was in Kinshasa, Zaire, twenty years earlier. The one I had stayed in Liberia in 1971 had been quite attractive too.

The irony is that in so called "third-world countries," such as the Congo, Colombia, India, Iran, Indonesia and Saudi Arabia, I have found not only bigger rooms but, more importantly, the medical care received has been a more humane and gentler experience than anything I have ever encountered in dealing dozens of times with hospitals and doctors in the United States, with rare exceptions. (To say nothing of the very low fees charged for those services overseas, as well as the very reasonable cost of drugs, even imported drugs.) For the kind of treatment I have required, the routine has been the same everywhere in the world, but the human touch and kindness of the providers has been for me more noticeable in foreign lands. It is a pitiful thing in the United States to come to an emergency room and find that urgent attention is delayed while the patient or a relative is questioned as to his or her insurance or financial solvency and then assumes and signs responsibility for payment of services. I don't remember the matter of money being the first question they asked overseas, ever.

In five days I was discharged from the hospital, having made a gradual and restful recovery with the dedicated and caring help of two doctors and many fine nurses. The doctors spoke some English, but the nurses knew very little. In spite of that we were able to communicate in my pidgin Indonesian and their pidgin English, and it was fun to try. In the tens of hospitals around the world where I have been treated, I have never known people with hands more gentle than those of the Indonesian health care professionals; they never, ever, failed to get the right vein on the first trial. Dreadful procedures like pricking deep in the tip of the fingers to measure gasses, something every asthmatic patient has to endure in a hospital, were inexplicably pain-less and, again, done right on the first trial.

My husband's bosses at the U. S. embassy in Jakarta were not amused about my emergency. They wired mes-sages to the Defense Language Institute's personnel office at Lackland Air Force Base, asking why they had sent this employee with an asthmatic wife overseas, threatening to send us back if any more problems arose about my condi-tion. Their concerns seemed rather hypocritical to me, since I was sure among the hundreds of embassy employ-ees and their dependents, there had to be a few asthmatics. One of my husband's bosses, a colonel, had told me, when I had inquired about medical facilities in Java months before, that there were an adequate number of doctors and hospitals in the main cities, and added that he himself suf-fered from high blood pressure and worried about his heart, and was taking medication for it. He had also informed me that sometimes patients who needed more sophisticated treatment had to hop to Singapore to get it. We had not kept any secrets from my husband's employers at Lackland, and they must have had records of the two medical evacuations the government had paid for in the past, one of them involving the use of a C-141 Air Force plane, while in the Congo, and possibly about my being hospitalized in Saudi Arabia. I knew that my family and I wanted to stay in Indonesia, and I prayed about it. All harassment died out.

With a group of interested foreign women, we organized a Yoga class, with a Hindu nun from Ananda Marga[15] as our teacher. The nun, a middle-aged Polish woman in her

---

[15] *A world wide religious organization founded by Prabhat Ranjan Sarkar, with head-quarters in Calcutta, India.*

orange habit, came once a week to give us a two-hour class at a friend's house. The 10-12 students in the class were foreign women from Australia, Canada, France, India, Korea, the United States, and me, a Colombian. The nun and I became very good friends. She was a very compassionate person who as a child in Poland during World War II had been a sickly, asthmatic, little girl. She was knowledgeable about natural medicine and taught me how to use the Bach flower remedies, as well as the principles of Indian Ayurvedic medicine. She also designed some special Yoga exercises to strengthen my lungs and respiratory system.

In August 1990 our son Christopher started classes at a missionary boarding school in the nearby town of Salatiga. The school had been established years before to educate missionary children but for several years had been accepting other English-speaking students living in neighboring towns. There were American, Australian, Indian, Korean and Japanese students, many of them the children of foreign businessmen in the region. The school was accredited in the U.S. and well staffed, covering grades 1-12. The spacious brand-new campus and dormitories housed more than a hundred boys and girls of all school ages that semester. The arrangement was very convenient for us, since Chris would be able to come home every weekend and then go back to school early Monday morning. And it was cheaper and closer than the international school in Jakarta the embassy had proposed. Besides, we though some religious education in the missionary school would be good for a sixteen-year-old boy. About a dozen students made the two-hour trip to Salatiga from our city every Monday.

# Chapter 22

# The Power of Prayer

It was in the small town of Salatiga that I had another close call in September 1991. My son had stayed home at the beginning of the week with a bad cold, but by Tuesday afternoon he felt well enough to go back to school, which meant that he would have to take a bus. To take a taxi would be rather expensive since we would have to pay the driver double fare to cover for his probably empty taxi back, so I decided to go to downtown Yogya with Chris to help him take an inter-city bus to Salatiga. But there was no direct bus leaving that afternoon for Salatiga. He could take one bus as far as the outskirts of Solo, a town a little more than an hour away, and then transfer there to another bus. My son dragged his feet about having to transfer midway, with the excuse that he might miss the transfer point and get lost. I ended up taking the bus with him to the next town, with the intention of returning as soon as he caught the right bus to school.

Trouble started just before arriving in Solo. I couldn't breathe well at all, and the inhaler I had with me was not giving me much relief. I had forgotten to take my Theophylline, and had none with me. We had to make a decision right away, either to go back home or to continue on to Salatiga, where I could buy the medicine I needed (prescriptions were often not asked for), rest until the attack subsided and, if necessary, spend the night at his school. The appearance of the Salatiga bus right then helped us make up our minds.

Seated at the back of the bus, a very large one without air-conditioning, people in the back soon noticed my distress and opened windows to let more air in. I was feeling more and more asphyxiated as the bus wound around the mountains towards Salatiga. Someone told the driver there was an emergency in the back of the bus and to hurry up. I prayed all the way and tried all the breathing tricks I knew. I am sure those in the bus prayed, too.

We barely made it to Salatiga. My son knew an American family who lived on the main street, where the bus had to pass, and decided to get off at their house to ask for help. Mrs.Cockenhauer, a long-time resident of Indonesia, took me in her car to the local hospital, where I promptly received oxygen and an adrenaline shot. She translated the necessary information from my son to the doctor and nurses, and back to us. But the two medicines I was receiving at that moment would not, by themselves, bring down a severe asthma attack, and this one was very bad indeed. Theophylline in the vein and a respirator were essential in cases like this, but this little hospital had neither. Theophylline had to be purchased at a nearby pharmacy in order to put in an IV right away.

Mrs. Cockenhauer phoned my son's school and other missionary wives in town to ask for their prayers. My husband and older son in Yogya were also notified about the emergency by telephone.

In the meantime, my struggle for breath was intense and painful; I was asphyxiated to the brink of unconsciousness, and I knew very well that if I lost consciousness, death could follow any moment. While my body was going through this agony, my mind and soul were engaged in prayer and surrender to God. The doctor thought I might need to be transferred to a better hospital in a bigger town. Surabaya was not far, but for the moment traveling and moving me around was not advisable. Besides, my husband had not arrived yet.

Two more ladies came to the hospital within minutes: Mrs. Cox, an American nurse who worked as dorm mother at Chris's school and Mrs. Schmidt, another missionary's wife. All three women sat in my room in prayerful vigil for a long time. There is no doubt in my mind that the prayers helped as much or more than the treatment; I couldn't talk, but I could feel those prayers working in my muscles and my lungs, easing the pain and the spasm, as well as in my soul in the form of soothing and peaceful waves. Slowly my breathing became less labored and quieter.

Of the many times I have been very sick in hospitals, I can recall two other occasions when I felt prayer at work that strongly: once in San Antonio, before going to Indonesia, when we had our neighborhood Catholic church, as well as some Baptist friends praying for me as I laid in the intensive care unit of a hospital in San Antonio, and again in San Antonio in 1994 when my husband had made a call to a nun and a priest, friends of ours, before getting in the car to follow the ambulance to the hospital. Our friends didn't mind that they were awakened late at night and said they would be praying right away. Again, I remember how much easier those first hours of hospitalization were for me than the times when nobody else was aware of my troubles or prayed. Then, as now, I had felt those prayers work on my flesh as well as my soul.

My husband arrived in Salatiga by taxi in the afternoon, bringing with him my nebulizer, a piece of equipment the hospital there didn't have, in order to take periodic therapy with it. He slept that night under my tall, rustic hospital bed, on a mat one of the missionary ladies had loaned him. His loving presence has always been an important factor in my recovery. He has been a husband, a nurse, a mother, a friend and everything good to me. In more than twenty-five years of dealing with this unpredictable and cruel illness, I have never heard him utter a complaint about my troubles.

Something of a coincidence or an act of intuition had happened that morning at home in Yogya. My husband on his way out to work had slipped a small photocopy of the Unity Church "Prayer for Protection" in his briefcase, a thing he is not in the habit of doing. When our older son called him at work in the afternoon to say that I had had an asthma attack and had been hospitalized in Salatiga, as he got ready to leave he noticed this singularly fitting prayer and read it with my safety in mind. On the way to Salatiga he repeated that prayer many times. It reads like this:

> PRAYER FOR PROTECTION
> The light of God surrounds us;
> The love of God enfolds us;
> The power of God protects us;
> The presence of God watches over us.
> Wherever we are, God is!

Twenty-four hours after my admission to the hospital, I was discharged to go home and continue treatment. The total cost of my 24-hour stay, including some medicines and the doctor's fee, was the paltry amount of $14.50. Being sick is not fun anywhere on earth, but if you get sick in Indonesia it will cost you very little money to see a doctor. In 1992 private doctors in a big city such as Yogyakarta charged from U.S. $2.00 to U.S. $2.50 per visit, and public hospitals and clinics charged as little as $0.75 per consultation. Also, you would get more time on a regular visit, than the 10-15 minutes the average doctor in the United States actually spends with you.

I am talking from experience. I have needed medical care all over the world (Colombia, Iran, India, Indonesia, Liberia, Saudi Arabia, Germany, the Congo and the United States). And for my health problems (mainly severe asthma), I have found medical attention overseas to be efficient, more compassionate and gentle, and less greedy than any medical service I have received in the United States.

# Chapter 23

# The Ripples of War

On January 17, 1991 (there is a twelve hour difference in time) we were unpleasantly surprised by the news of war breaking out in the Middle East. We had followed with interest the conflict between Iraq and Kuwait in the last part of 1990 and had hoped for a peaceful, diplomatic solution, but by early January an attack on Iraq seemed imminent. My husband got the news as he arrived at the U.S. embassy in Jakarta that Thursday morning, on the second day of his routine monthly trip to the capital, and an Indonesian secretary said to him, "There is bad news." Later he heard reports of massive air attacks on Iraq, on CNN at the embassy cafeteria. "Most Americans here seem pleased," he observed in his diary.

I was at home in Yogyakarta when I heard the news from London on the BBC. There is no joy in hearing about war; I wept at the inhumanity of it. "Air attacks" meant bombs, and bombs are not rose petals, they mean death and destruction. As I sat alone in the sitting room, I heard the clowns tell me, "It will be a short war, but they will be at it again soon." And it was so. Defeat after defeat Saddam Hussein rose again and again in defiance. (Here we are, November 17, 1997 as I write this paragraph, and they are at it again. The threat of war is hanging over us once more.)

The foreign community in Indonesia became quite concerned at that time. Living in the largest Islamic country in the world, nobody was sure how the Indonesians would react to the allied forces' attack on Iraq. We did the prudent thing and kept a low profile for the first few days, waiting for any signs of unrest. None occurred in Yogya. In Jakarta, however, there were a few demonstrations against the United States, and a bomb was found on the grounds of the U.S. ambassador's residence on January 18th.

The embassy instructed us not to go to Jakarta in case of danger, but to get to the island of Bali (where the population is mostly Hindu) instead, and from there catch a flight to either Australia or the Philippines. Local Indonesian Air Force officials assured my husband they would provide any support needed. Fortunately, things stayed calm in Yogya and in Central Java in general.

A few weeks into the Gulf War my husband had to go on TDY (temporary duty) to Bandung, on the northwest coast of Java. He noticed at that time he was the only non-Asian foreigner on the flight, which under ordinary circumstances would have been quite unusual. It seems that westerners were still exercising caution in traveling around the country.

The Gulf War proved quite detrimental to Indonesia as far as tourism was concerned. Foreign visitors, who were expected to visit the country in record numbers in 1991, stayed away most of the year. Very few (mostly Australians) trickled down through the ancient city of Yogya where we lived. The costly "Visit Indonesia Year 1991" campaign did very little to reassure foreign travelers that Indonesia was safe.

## Chapter 24

# Other Lands, Other Lives

On my second trip to Spain, in April 1983, accompanied by a lady friend from the U.S. Military Training Mission in Riyadh, Saudi Arabia and her 15-year-old daughter, we visited the Museo del Prado in Madrid and several other tourist attractions in the capital and in nearby towns, including my favorite one, Toledo, and then headed south for the warmer climate of Andalusia.

On a visit to El Escorial[16], some thirty miles away from Madrid, while walking through that massive building, a strange feeling began to arise within me. My eyes found the place a little bit oppressive (not enough light in it, for one thing), but my soul was in a reverie. The engineering prodigy before my eyes, made me weep and thank God for man's divinity. Then, as I stood glued to the floor across from the altar of the small chapel inside the palace, a small voice sounded inside me: "And you had a lot to do with it," then the words, "the architect." By then my friends had moved to another section of the building, unaware of the motive for my staying behind. Summoning my reasoning and skeptical mind to my aid, I shook my head and continued the tour without further interference.

I have had the tendency to stop strange occurrences like that in the middle of the way, when my rational mind cannot understand them, or out of fear, or whatever. Once, at age ten, while in church in my hometown of Falan

---

[16] *Built in the 16th century under Philip II as a residence, a monastery, and a mausoleum for his father Charles V. Other Spanish kings are also buried there.*

(Colombia), as I was kneeling in prayer, everything began to turn around, faster and faster, and I started to levitate from the kneeling board, while a statue of St. Anne (the patroness saint of my town), placed in a niche some fifteen feet away, began to move its mouth as if saying something. I held on with my hands to the back of the bench in front of me and said "What is this?" The experience ended right away, and I sat for a long while not knowing what to think of it. As a child, too, going to class one day, carrying my violin (in its case), on an uphill street, I felt I wasn't walking on the ground but floating fast, a few feet off the ground, straight ahead in the general direction I was going. The moment I realized I was flying, not walking, I gently descended to the sidewalk again, asking myself how that had happened.

Another spontaneous psychic experience took place in Indonesia in late 1991. My husband's supervisor had come from Jakarta one weekend and we thought of inviting her to visit Prambanan, a beautiful complex of ancient Hindu temples and ruins, dating from the 9th century and located about 15 kilometers from Yogya, which we had observed from the distance many times in route to the nearby towns of Solo and Salatiga but never visited.

The Prambanan complex contains more than a dozen temples of different sizes, the tallest one measuring 170 feet. A vast area of ruins lies near the temples, awaiting reconstruction. The three main temples, intended as earthly replicas of heavenly mansions, are dedicated to the Hindu Trinity: Brahma, the creator; Visnu, the preserver; and Shiva, the destroyer. These temples are considered the most graceful examples of Hindu architecture in Indonesia. There are nine smaller temples surrounding the three larger ones, and many more minor shrines are being reconstructed from the extensive ruins, with great patience and dedication, by specialists under the auspices of the Indonesian government. Construction of the temple complex started in 856 AD, and when it was finished, about a hundred years later, it included the three main temples plus 224 of the smaller size shrines, monasteries, hostels and administration facilities. The complex was partially destroyed in 1584 by an eruption of nearby Mount Merapi, and suffered considerable damage in 1967 during an earthquake.

That Saturday afternoon we took a taxi to the site, bought our tickets and started walking towards the ruins. As I handed my ticket to the ticket taker at the entrance and crossed the gate into the temple grounds, a stabbing pain in my stomach made me gasp. I managed to control myself and go on with the tour. The pain varied in intensity as I walked around; I did not feel too much pain climbing several flights of stairs to each of the three main temples, inside the temples, or climbing down from them. But walking around a large stretch of the complex and also near the entrance walls, the pain was almost unbearable, and I was close to tears. We did the tour of the ruins and temples in about two hours, finding the buildings amazingly beautiful, and then headed for the souvenir shops, just outside the entrance gate.

As I approached the gate to exit the complex, the pain intensified, and then as I stepped outside the gate, it suddenly stopped, completely. My stomach felt fine from then on. This strange event made me very curious to find out why I had felt that way in a place where I had gone as an unbiased tourist and nothing else. I knew I had to go back and discover what was there that affected me so badly.

On December 9, 1991 (a Sunday), there were two strong earth tremors, a few minutes apart, in Yogyakarta. After we calmed down, I thought I should go to Prambanan again, before Mount Merapi erupted (the nearby volcano had been fuming for years), or another earthquake damaged the temples. But the strangest thing happened just the moment I thought about going back to Prambanan: My stomach started hurting again with a sharp pain, and I said, "No, it can't be," "I won't allow it!" And I stopped it. I felt even more determined to go back to the temples right away. With my husband and our two sons, we took a taxi and left for the complex.

It was a cloudy day and, being monsoon season, we had taken our umbrellas with us. As we entered the temple complex, the pain in my stomach attacked me once more as it had done during my first visit, but this time it made me bend over with pain as I clutched a folded umbrella against my chest. A flood of tears followed. I sat on a pile of stones and cried, as I never had before, for at least twenty minutes, unable to stop. Later, as I moved away from the section that seemed to be the center of the strange disturbance to my body and spirit, we were able to show our boys the beautiful temples and explain to them the meaning of some of the statues and symbols on the altars and decorations that we were familiar with, such as the story of Ganesha, the elephant god.

I decided to come back a third time, but on a weekday when there wouldn't be any large crowds to distract me, or the boys to get annoyed at me, and do a meditation to try to find out what was bothering me in that place, which otherwise was so lovely.

The third time, my husband and I headed directly for one of the troublesome spots, and I still had to weep some more. Then, I sat down, closed my eyes and went into meditation. Within minutes there was a passing vision inside my closed eyes, like the movement of a movie camera, and a voice saying: "Yes, it was violent death for you and your family." "You were a man then, an administrator; you fought bravely, but it was a slaughter." "You didn't mind dying yourself, but you saw everyone being killed, your dear family and about a hundred others." "This family?" I asked. The voice replied, "Not this husband; not your children, but you know some of them now; one of your brothers." "Which one," I asked. "You will know in a dream," the voice replied. "And you should come here again; it will be less painful every time," it said. Sandy ground was the last thing I saw before the vision faded. I finished my meditation, feeling quite at peace.

This revelation was of great relief to me; I understood that the history of the place, including the love of countless worshipers and the hatred and envy of enemies, had stayed imprinted everywhere at that complex, and that my presence there had awakened soul memories in me, too.

In a seemingly unrelated way, while still around the temples, I thought about an elderly lady I had met at Bible classes in San Antonio some years before, remembering that just after I had met her I had looked in her eyes and had told her: "Harriet, you were very important and dear to me ages ago." Why was I remembering this incident now? As told in the vision, she must have been one of those I had known at Prambanan. About the brother the voice had mentioned, months later, back in the United States, I had a dream in which a handsome young man had turned into my brother Ivan, and someone had asked, "Have you told Ivan about Prambanan?" This brother is 12 years younger than I, and yes, very handsome. Of my seven brothers and sisters, he was my favorite while growing up. I wanted to take care of him, to dress him the best, to take him places, to give him music lessons; in a word, I loved him deeply. He must have been the one I had known in that lifetime, too.

I visited Prambanan a total of five times, the last two in January 1992 with visiting friends from Hawaii, and in February of the same year, just a few weeks before our return to the United States. As advised in the vision, every visit to the complex became a little easier.

On my last visit to Prambanan I wanted to take into my heart for the last time the imposing beauty of that place, and to say good-bye to it in love, reverence and gratitude. I had commented to my husband that I had not cried that day at all, and asked him to take one last picture. We moved towards some ruins not far from the exit, and as I leaned on a pile of heavy black blocks of carved stone, the pain hit me once again. I asked him to take the picture quickly, and when I stepped aside, the pain subsided. I then took a picture of my husband leaning on the same stones, but he didn't feel a thing. The picture he took of me at that spot shows my grimacing face as pain got hold of me one last time.

With age and the many unusual things I have seen so far, I have learned to be more accepting and receptive to all the goodness God wants to show me (in as many manifestations as He wants to use), and to help others in any way I can. Still, those who know me best, sometimes point to my denials and reluctance to fully embrace my life with its strange gifts and pain. But sometimes I am confused; it is like having a job and not knowing the description of your duties and your schedule; and then there is my impatience and, of course, the ever present obstacle of this unremitting illness. I sometimes console myself by thinking about the great saints in the world. They didn't have it easy either; their lives were not a "bed of roses"; many of them were racked with illness, yet work they did. I can think of my favorite ones such as St. Francis of Assisi, Hildegard von Bingen, St. Theresa of Jesus, or Mother Theresa of Calcutta, and then I bless God for the beauty of their lives and say to myself: "Gloria, stop whimpering about your life, this is peanuts; you are a hardy soul, too!"

Right after our return from Indonesia in March 1992, on a whim, I went to a psychic fair, at a mall near my home. Several psychics were giving free demonstrations of their skills to the visitors. I decided to kind of test a graphologist first, expecting some nonsense, but I was pleasantly impressed by her analysis of the paragraph I had written. Some of my character traits were accurately described from my handwriting. I thanked her for her job. What really surprised me next was the palm reader's free sample. She took my hand in her hands and blurted: "Goodness! You are here by divine intervention. You have seen it this close," and put her extended hand in front of her nose and eyes. Then continued, "You have been very sick and could have died three different times." "You must have something important to do here." I told her she must really know her stuff, because that was a close description of my three NDEs. She smiled and said, "It's all there," and showed me the three disconnected lines (instead of one continuous one) that form my lifeline, rubbing her finger on the lines. Sure enough that is how both of my palms are marked.

**Chapter 25**

# A Long Relationship with Death

To say that I have had a long relationship with death is an understatement. Death and the symbols of death have been around me since childhood. The first symbol of death came to me at age five in the form of a specific flowery perfume that I still call "the smell of death." It is the oldest of the gift of fragrances that has been bestowed upon me and, like the other three perfumes I smell, it is very dear to me.

Death itself would become a familiar sight early in my life, and I knew when it was coming before we became aware of its sad reality, because the "perfume of death" was in the air ahead of time, and I could sense it. Other symbols of death appeared in the form of apparitions at ages eight, ten and eleven, as described in later chapters. As a child in my hometown of Falan, Colombia, the late 1940s and early 1950s were times of violence and horror. An undeclared civil war was raging across the country, carried on, initially, by the ruling political party against towns and citizens sympathizing with the opposition, and then, by both sides in a blood bath that took more than 100 thousand lives in five years of power struggle.

My hometown, too, was caught in the senseless hatred that followed the "Bogotazo," a bloody revolt in April 1948, following the assassination of Jorge Eliecer Gaitan, one of the two liberal presidential candidates in the 1946 elections, which the liberals had lost to the single conservative candidate. Being only six hours away from Bogotá, the capital of Colombia, my town, which had supported the popular, assassinated candidate, was targeted by the conservative government for retaliation. Hundreds of men, women and children, mostly peasants living in small agricultural communities outside of town, were murdered. Trucks full of police coming from the capital were responsible for the first raids and atrocities against the innocent peasants. Our town, with about 17,500 people, was too big for the official thugs to do their misdeeds unopposed, but it wasn't completely immune. Some of the dead were brought to town to be buried, some were buried on their own farms.

My parents did what they could to keep me and my little brothers from learning what was going on, but the "perfume of death" would alert and sadden me. Besides, sometimes I couldn't help hearing from other adults and children some gross details of the massacres, and to notice the unusual number of funerals that were taking place in town. There was also a fearful atmosphere that was hard to ignore, especially on Sunday afternoons when the main streets and plaza would be empty earlier than usual. An open market was held at the main plaza on Sundays, but all stands would be closed by three instead of five in the afternoon, because the citizens feared the policemen (all strangers to the townspeople) would get drunk and go on a rampage anywhere in town. That, of course, had happened already, when drunken policemen had killed three men in a bar, one of them the husband of one of my aunts.

To a sensitive seven-year-old like me, no amount of parental reassurance was enough to stop my worries. Passing near those rifle-carrying policemen in green uniforms, on my way to school, to the stores, or to church, was very stressful. I remember telling myself: "Walk very fast now Gloria, and don't look at them." In my married life, when my husband joined the U.S. Air Force reserve in San Antonio in 1977, many times, seeing him in his green fatigue uniform, I felt irrationally repulsed. He ended up resigning his two-year agreement with the reserve after about a year of service. I am very sure the sight of him in his green uniform triggered that feeling of repulsion I had felt as a child, even though my husband had chosen to serve in a medical evacuation unit. My younger son is now in the Army reserve, but his camouflage fatigues haven't affected me in the same way.

## Chapter 26

# A Child's Vision

Between the ages of seven and eight, I had my first vision related to death. One evening before going to bed early, as children did fifty years ago when there was no television to distract them, the sun had gone down already and I was sitting in the kitchen reading to the light of a low-power light bulb hanging low from the wall. I was facing the back patio through an open door, when something caught my attention. Some twenty feet away, close to a barbwire fence dividing our house from a public school's grounds, there was a small white coffin floating in the air. It changed position from a side view to a full top view, as if invisible hands were showing it to me. I jumped out of my chair, dropped the book and ran to another room screaming. My parents came to inspect the spot and tried to comfort and convince me that there was nothing there. From then on I did my reading somewhere else in the house.

The grounds where the school was located had a history of ghosts and hauntings, but we didn't personally know anybody who had seen the spooks – just stories of the past and hearsay. What was well known was the fact that at the turn of the century, during the "guerra de los mil dias" (the thousand-day war), a hospital and a cemetery had occupied that land, including the place where our neighbor's house and ours were now standing. That might explain the kind of apparition I saw that night and the one more I relate in the next chapter, involving symbols of death.

One of my youngest brothers did see, years later, something very scary around our house when he was barely three years old. Some animal-like creature had placed itself between his legs, grown bigger and carried him on its back a distance. We found the child holding onto a table in the open corridor of the house, screaming: "*Me caigo, me caigo!*" (I am falling, I am falling!) He was very pale and about to faint. Later he described the best he could what had scared him so badly.

Because of the violence and danger in my hometown in those years, in 1951, my parents decided to send me to live in Bogotá with one of my father's brothers and his family; I was ten years old. Many women and even little girls had been raped in the region where we lived and, being a girl, my parents feared for my safety. I was the oldest of six children; after me came three brothers, and my two sisters, one two years old and the youngest a few months old. Two more brothers were born later. It was a painful decision for my parents and for me to be separated at such an early age. My father visited me several times a year, and I cried a lot after his visits. I was allowed to spend a few weeks at Christmas time in my hometown with my parents and siblings, which did a lot to restore my spirits. Then, in January, I would go back to Bogotá for another year of school.

## Chapter 27

# Another Apparition

My grandmother, on my father's side, had been a baker all her life, but now living by herself, since two grand-daughters she had raised were married and gone, she couldn't keep up with the demand for baked goods from her customers. My mother had taken over part of the baking business my grandma could not take care of.

One Wednesday morning in December of 1951, while I was back home after a year in the capital, my mother and I had gotten up at five a.m. to cook lunch for two workers at our farm to take along, and to start making the bread for a couple of corner stores she had agreed to supply twice a week. It was still dark, and I was filling up a bucket with water from the faucet located outside the kitchen (there was no running water in the kitchen), when, out of the corner of my eye, I noticed a light moving behind me. I turned around and saw a candle, tall and thick, like those they light for Easter in the church, floating straight in the air, roughly in the same place where more than a year earlier I had seen a little white coffin.

I ran into the kitchen where my mother was working, very, very scared. My mother hugged me and tried to calm me down, but she wouldn't dare to go and look at the apparition. She said it was probably just a twig or a stick shining in the moonlight and promised to go out there with me and look, as soon as there was sunlight. And we did, but there was nothing sticking up, not even weeds, since they appeared to have been recently cut.

# Chapter 28

# A Man in White

By the end of January 1952, I was back in Bogotá to start the school year, which ran from February to mid-June and then from August to mid-December. That year my father had made arrangements for me to board with a sister of his and her family. My aunt was a good woman, but stern and hot-tempered like my father. She and her husband, a professional photographer, owned a large two-story house, which they shared with my uncle's mother, a son and a daughter close to my age. This was my second year away from home; by then I was getting more used to it and, as usual, was doing well in school.

My aunt's mother-in-law, Mrs. O., and I shared one of the two rooms on the first floor, next to the kitchen, facing a long patio full of geraniums and azaleas growing in pots. Mrs. O. was a gentle woman and a devout Catholic who liked to attend the earliest of the Sunday masses at the neighborhood church, at six a.m. I sometimes accompanied her to mass. One Sunday morning in June, Mrs. O. asked me if I wanted to go to mass with her, but I told her I'd rather sleep a little more. She left for church alone at about 5:30 a.m. I closed my eyes and tried to go back to sleep, but a moment later I felt something cold touch my forehead. I opened my eyes to see a man, all in white, turn around and leave my bedside. Thinking it was a burglar, I threw my covers down and went after him. As I came through my bedroom door, I could still see his back as he moved quickly among the plants, then, suddenly, he puffed into thin air. At this point I felt my hair stand on end, and I ran towards my cousin's room, to pound desperately on his door. He got up upset at me for waking him up and asked what all that noise was about. In tears, I related to him what I had just seen, and as I recalled the cold touch to my forehead, I felt goose bumps all over my body. My cousin made light of it and told me I had probably had a bad dream. A long time passed before I dared to go outside my room after dark again.

I returned to my hometown at the end of the year (1952) for my school vacation and to meet my new brother, Ivan, who had been born in early November. The town had enjoyed about half a year of relative peace, and my parents considered it safe for me to stay home with my family to attend a coeducational private high school, which had just ended its first year of operation in town. (There is no middle school in Colombia. After five years of elementary school, you go to high school for six more years.)

The political situation improved even more after June 1953 when the conservative government was overthrown by General Rojas Pinilla, who declared himself president and soon after that declared a general amnesty for the fighting political factions in the country. (He became the second dictator in the history of my country after its independence from Spain in 1810, and the only one in this twentieth century.) Rojas Pinilla's dictatorship lasted four years. In May 1957 his government was, in turn, overthrown by a military junta, which ruled temporarily until a pact between the two traditional parties (liberal and conservative) was made in 1958, agreeing to govern by turns for periods of four years each during the next sixteen years.

Life in a small town is never too complicated, and I settled into my routine of studying, helping at home with the bakery business and helping my father, who was a small merchant, in his business on weekends. My father was an occasional correspondent for the two main national daily newspapers, El Tiempo and El Espectador, published in Bogotá, and he distributed those and some national magazines, as well as comics and other international publications such as Life magazine and Reader's Digest (in Spanish translations), plus at least three state lotteries to our town and two neighboring ones. Thanks in part to my father's love for the written word, we were in those years a well-informed little town.

Some of the finest literary masterpieces were also available to me from two sources: the town priest, who kindly opened his private library to the high school I was attending (he taught a weekly class there on morality and religion) and my grandfather on my mother's side, who was a music lover and owned a good number of fine musical and literary works. I became acquainted with Dante, Cervantes, Chateubriand, Goethe and others in my early teens.

Violin lessons were also part of my youth. In relation to music, something very amusing happened when I was a little baby. My parents had an ocelot before I was born and had kept the animal after I was born. But maybe because of his nature or because he felt neglected, the feline became fond of killing chickens, around the time I was starting to crawl. My parents decided to get rid of the ocelot, but the best deal they could find was to trade it for a violin. Thus we got ourselves a violin. My father was somewhat artistic and in his twenties had toured with a zarzuela[17] group (not a soloist). He was fond of singing, but not overly so. Bad temper was his most notable trait, unfortunately.

About my father's character, I have to recognize that he was a good provider for his family and a generous and helpful man to others. But his bad moments were too many and too often around us. The older children, especially myself and the three that followed, suffered innumerable whippings from him, so many, that the three boys ran away from home, at least twice each one, before the age of fifteen. Had I been a boy I would have done the same. Instead, many times I wished him dead and started to pile up a lot of anger towards him. My mother would try to defend us as much as she could, if she was around, sometimes getting hit in the process, until she was able to subdue him. (My father had learned not to mess with her early in their married life when she had responded to his attack by throwing him on the floor and trying to choke him.) By today's standards and even then, he would be considered an abusive father.

I really thought my father hated me, but filling my heart with more anger or hatred towards him didn't seem right. After a long self-examination, at age fifteen, I felt I had had enough of those nasty feelings towards my father and decided to do my part, regardless of his behavior and at least try not to hate him. Magical things happened: unexpectedly people began to tell me how proud and grateful my father was to have me as a daughter, and about all the other fine things he had to say about me. I was amazed to hear that and began to see him with kinder eyes and to observe that the poor man just didn't have the capacity to

---

[17] *Spanish operetta or musical comedy (Velazquez Spanish and English Dictionary).*

express his love for us in a better way. I felt sorry for him and had much more understanding for him from then on.

My relationship with my father slowly developed to a satisfactory level, but it was never affectionate. I accepted him with his human flaws and myself with mine, while trying to accommodate to his ways without bending mine too much.

My change of heart regarding my father had some spiritual repercussions I had not foreseen. My religious beliefs until that time had been based on the teachings of the Catholic Church I had been born into, but now waves of questioning, doubt and dissatisfaction began to lash at my soul. For one thing, I found no justification for the suffering of innocent children, for their hunger and disease and for their dying before fulfilling their potential. Wars, natural disasters and accidents that befell good people, seemed unwarranted, too. Where was God, I asked myself, or is He so blind and cruel that he allows all this horror to tear at us helpless creatures? The Church advised patience, acceptance and obedience to God's will, but these mandates seemed to me empty and heartless. I would not be part of that. I left the Church I had loved as a child, to look for answers elsewhere.

Help came promptly in the form of an old man who called himself an atheist but had much kindness and wisdom to give to others, if they ever asked. He was my godmother's older brother, a widower and a carpenter by trade. He had been a Rosicrusian, well acquainted with the doctrine of reincarnation, which he explained to me in several talks. What a revelation! It made so much sense to me, to know that we humans don't ever see the whole picture, just our human nature and the events of our present incarnation, and therefore, can not judge on the reasons and justice for the harshness and trials we encounter. The causes are probably of our own making, and the circumstances of our present lives chosen just to help us learn necessary lessons for our soul's development. I was grateful that I had encountered him early enough, because with his help I was able to get rid of some useless religious baggage and start my spiritual search early on.

My country's conscience was also being stirred at that time. By mid 1956 dissatisfaction with the military dictator Rojas Pinilla was on the rise and guerrillas were roaming the countryside again. We were aware of the danger of an attack on the town, where young men and the police station would be possible targets, since the guerrillas wanted men and arms to enlarge its numbers. My parents with one teenage boy (fourteen), plus their concern for me and the rest of the brood, decided to move to the capital. But it would take some time for my father to sell at least the house, or the farm, since the family didn't have much in the way of savings. I was sent ahead to Bogotá in November of that year to live with relatives.

Before the year was over, I had found a job as a secretary at a law firm. Fortunately, along with my academic studies, I had learned to type, and that plus a certain air of self-confidence they saw in me, convinced my would be bosses to give me the job. After three months of evening shorthand classes, I received my first raise in salary just before my sixteenth birthday.

Seven months after my arrival, my parents along with my other seven brothers and sisters joined me in Bogotá. The small farm my father had outside of Falan had been sold, but the money was not enough to get us a house in the capital. So we had to make do with a rented apartment. Eight children didn't make it easy to find many landlords willing to rent to us, we found out. Soon my father opened a tiny corner store, with rather sparse merchandise but enough to give us a lean income.

While working as a secretary, my attention turned to the study of foreign languages. I decided to start evening English classes at the U.S. bi-national center, where years later my husband would be teaching. In three years of studies I took every class they had to offer, including some basic English literature. French, Italian and Russian occupied most of my after-work hours for the next six years. For a while I considered going to Moscow on a scholarship to study medicine, but on closer examination I realized I couldn't stand some of the grosser aspects of the training. Besides language studies, I was part of the choir at the National Conservatory, where I had studied the violin earlier, and my seven-year-old brother Ivan was now beginning music lessons. It was a very full schedule for me, but that was the way I liked it.

About boyfriends, I didn't have much time for them. My father was lucky I wasn't fond of parties or boy crazy, or we would have been at each other's throats more than once. However, I was always in love with somebody, mostly classmates or teachers, though at a distance. He had been impolite once to a young neighbor I liked, who had walked me to my house a few times. Although embarrassed, I didn't think the feeling was strong enough to fight for it, yet. I did give my father some heartache just before his death when I fell in love with a cousin and my father thought we might get married. We enjoyed each other's company and affection but the relationship was not serious enough to talk marriage. The fact that we were first cousins never bothered us, but it worried our families a great deal. My father died in 1965 of lung cancer at age 60; he had been a smoker for fifty years. His stubbornness showed to the end, when he said to us that he would wait until his sixtieth birthday to die. Although he was hopelessly sick, in great pain and reduced to just a living skeleton, he managed to hold on until the 31st of July (his birthday), dying in his sleep the morning of August 1, 1965.

The work of the subconscious mind is an amazing thing. Shortly after my father's death I had a most uncomfortable dream, an exaggerated play on reality. *I dreamed that my father was lying in a coffin and my mother and I were busy nailing it shut while he tried to resist by pushing the cover with his outstretched hands.* End of the dream. Cruel as the dream was, I knew in my heart that his death would be in a real way a liberating experience for my mother and me, because at times we had felt quite oppressed by him.

## Chapter 29

# A Soul Call for a Good Man

Approaching my twenty-fifth birthday, I started to ask myself what I wanted to do with my life, and found two things at the top of the list I would like to tackle: traveling, which I had day-dreamed about many times in my youth, and finding an ideal man to share my life with. After a close inventory, I couldn't find a truly suitable man among my few wooers of the last three years. Two were too conservative, one too rude, and another, my cousin, had a wandering eye for other women; I knew a marriage to any of these men wouldn't last long at all. (My thinking wasn't far off; to this date my cousin, the only one I had heard about since then, has been married three times). I settled for traveling first and seeking a husband later.

I asked God to send my way the best possible husband, and then made plans for traveling within a year, first to Peru to see Machu Pichu and then to Europe. I purchased a ticket on the installment plan to make it easy on my pocket and to give myself time to save a little more money for expenses. I had a good job in the publicity department of a well-known international Dutch company, and the work was varied and satisfying, but my "itchy feet" could not wait much longer; I would leave for Peru by December 1966.

The love of my life (my husband Cliff) showed up in June 1966, a few months before my departure date for Peru. Born in Detroit and raised in Florida, he too had had plans for traveling. After graduating from Florida State

University with a major in German, he had taught high school in southwest Nebraska for one year and then had gone to Germany to work during the summer of 1965. But the cold, gloomy weather he found in Nuremberg that year was not exactly to his liking. Remembering that he had friends with the Peace Corps working in Colombia, he decided to go pay them a visit and enjoy the warmth of the tropics at the same time. He promptly quit his job, went to Antwerp, Belgium and caught a German freighter bound for Colombia, arriving in Barranquilla in the fall of 1965.

Inquiring about his friends, in Bogotá, Cliff found out that they had already completed their assignment in Colombia and had left the country. Still it was tempting for him to stay a little longer and see more of the country. But with money running out, he would need at least a short-term job. Why not try that? He found cheaper accommodations at a boarding house owned by an old German and his Colombian wife, a clean place frequented by Peace Corps volunteers and other wandering foreigners with little money. In no time he also found a part-time teaching position at the U.S. sponsored bi-national center, the Centro Colombo-Americano, where nine years earlier I had studied English.

Cliff's roommate happened to be an English teacher at the Institute of Foreign Languages where I was doing my third year of Russian and beginning German at that time. Teachers talk among themselves about their students, and after five years of taking classes with some of them at the Institute, they liked me well. I had the reputation of being a good student and a serious young woman. Harold Schuller told me one day that his roommate (Cliff) was from the United States, handsome and single, spoke

German and was "like a monk." He then asked me if I would like to meet him. The part about being handsome and speaking German sounded interesting to me, and I agreed to meet his friend that weekend.

That Saturday afternoon in early June 1966, Harold introduced me to Cliff at a soda fountain, had a glass of juice with us and quickly disappeared. The first thing I noticed about Cliff was his deep, resonant voice and his slightly sad eyes. Conversation was easy, in a mixture of his rudimentary Spanish, my not so fluid English and probably a tad of German, not a problem at any moment. We walked to a park some ten blocks away and there walked some more, talked some more and took photographs. The next day we went to a museum he had some interest in seeing and did a few more miles of walking and talking. That became a routine for us in the following weekends.

It was not love at first sight for either one of us, but the love bug got to us very fast; I know it did to me. Being a veteran of falling in love and not telling, having the man so close to me this time, and doing all that talking and sharing was an improvement over the countless times I had been contented with a greeting and a smile from the men I secretly loved. My cousin I had held and kissed many times, but there was no soul communication to the degree that Cliff and I were finding together.

A tragedy that touched both of us in a slightly different way was the catalyst that brought our lives together faster in a more dramatic way than we had intended. In late August 1966 a terrorist bomb went off at the Centro Colombo-Americano where Cliff taught. Six people were killed, one American among them. The bomb had been hidden in a women's restroom on the first floor. Two minutes earlier, on the way to his classroom on the third floor, Cliff had just passed the area where the bomb went off. He was handing out papers to the students when it went off, shaking the whole building badly. All the windows on the first floor and many on the other floors were blown out. One of his students, arriving late, was hurt by flying glass. When the classrooms were evacuated, those on the two higher floors had to walk past the torn bodies of the dead.

I was working at my desk that afternoon, with the radio on as usual, when the normal program was interrupted with a news bulletin informing us of an explosion at the Centro Colombo-Americano. I thought of Cliff and prayed to God, "let him be well," or something of that sort. But mostly I thought of my friend Maria Eugenia, a few doors down the hall, whose husband was also working at the Colombo-Americano. I went to her office immediately to tell her about the news on the radio, but she thought I was pulling her leg. When she saw I was not kidding, we then searched for more news on the radio; the news was everywhere.

After several telephone calls, my friend learned that her husband had been "badly injured." (He had actually been killed instantly, as she would learn later.) Such grief for a wife, a bride of five months, as she was. The young man was a promising playwright and poet, in charge of the office of cultural activities at the Colombo.

I tried to locate Cliff and finally succeeded about two hours later. I wanted to see him to make sure he was okay. I saw him after work; so happy to hug him once more.

My friend Maria Eugenia was a secretary and an amateur theater performer. I had known her for about two years at work and had gotten to know her rather well with our frequent chats while riding the company bus to and from the same neighborhood. I don't remember if she called me, or I offered my help to make the funeral arrangements (after all I knew something about that from having lost my father a year earlier), but the next day the two of us were at the funeral parlor doing just that; it all seemed surreal. The important thing is that she got all the presence of mind she needed to deal with her situation.

The tragedy made Cliff realize how ephemeral life can be and the importance of making it worthwhile while it lasts. Marriage might have entered his mind already, but there was no urgency about it for either one of us, after only three months of knowing each other. Now that death had just shown its claws in front of us, it was time to make a choice for life, a life of sharing and discovery. A few days after, he proposed. Three months later, on Thanksgiving Day 1966, we got married.

The sale of the airline ticket I had been paying for got us some home utensils and a coat for my husband. I knew I would be traveling later, since Cliff had no plans to stay in Colombia permanently, just one more year to get to know some of the country, and my family, a little better. My plans for traveling had been reversed; by a divine twist I had gotten a husband first and through him, without knowing it, a ticket to see the world. More than thirty years later, I can't complain about that change.

# Chapter 30

# More Men in White

When I was touched on the forehead by the man in white, at age eleven, my main reaction was fear. The two apparitions at ages eight and ten had had the same effect in my mind; I was too young to fully understand the meaning in the symbols of the coffin and the candle, and the touch by the man in white. But after receiving more messages and initiations (especially from my early thirties on, after I came down with asthma), in the form of visions and dreams of an extraordinarily clear quality, clearer than daily life scenes, and then having had those three near-death experiences, I came to understand that I had been chosen early on for the work of the White Brotherhood on earth and in the spirit realms.

The work of the White Brotherhood covers all types of spiritual endeavors. It is all part of God's work, and it ranges from helping in the process of birthing, to making the transition at the moment of death, and every good work in between that man undertakes. On this earth too, people of good will and understanding can help the angelic forces do their work if they selflessly make themselves available to God in body, mind and spirit. The beauty of it is that we can do God's work not only in our waking life but even when we are asleep.

Throughout the years, I have seen many men in white in my dreams, and I see myself turning into a man in white to become one of them. I have worked with them in wars and famines, in refugee camps, helping souls cross the threshold of life onto the other side, encouraging, consoling and calming their minds as they embrace the new life. This is why, when the clowns said to me in the hospital in Pensacola: "We know you well, you are one of us," I knew they were referring to my spiritual work with the White Brotherhood.

In this "line of work" you answer when you are called and then you do your work with love, compassion and joy whether you are ushering one soul at the time, or walking with a group of them, up to a point, towards the light. As for helping members of my own family at the time of their passing, I have not been aware of it yet. My father died "on my watch," while I was asleep in the same room, but I don't recall my presence in the spirit world on that occasion. And, one of my cousins, who died young (and violently) almost twenty years ago, came back in my dreams months later to greet me and to tell me that he had missed me by his side when he had passed on, thousands of miles away. I am sure others were lovingly assisting him (as they assist everyone), although in the physical sense he had died a lonely death.

In December 1995 one of my younger son's friends died in a car accident in San Antonio. Tony was a member of the same band my son played with, a handsome struggling musician with a lot of talent and only nineteen years old. We were shocked when we heard the news; the young man had been at my house several times and seemed very likable. The next day, as I was going about my chores, I heard Tony's voice clearly, somewhere inside me, saying, "Call my mother, she needs comforting." I didn't know her well but had planned to go with my son and pay her a visit within the next few days. I phoned right away and repeated to her the words I had just heard. She was indeed deeply anguished about the circumstances of her son's death and the pain he must have suffered, his fears at the moment of death, his salvation etc. I tried to reassure her that the love and mercy of God would not fail His precious child, her child; we talked a fairly long time, relating to her my own experiences, which she found quite comforting. Tony's mother and I have become very good friends. After her son's passing she has gone on to experience extraordinary demonstrations of after-death communication with her son, like the one she witnessed at the cemetery months after his death when she asked for a sign that he was with her in spirit, and an Easter lily jumped from the vase on the tombstone to her feet, a yard or so away.

In retrospect I can see that my early acquaintance with the subject of death has served me well in my own three near-death experiences. My first NDE, for example, seemed to me an utterly natural process and, as if I were used to it, I even asked God for music. Those three experiences and earlier initiations have helped me to understand the work I do, which seems to include a variety of duties.

In waking life I pray daily for the dying and the sick, in general. But my prayers become more individualized whenever I sense the perfume of death around me or when I occasionally hear three urgent knocks, which has become another way of letting me know that somebody in particular is asking for a prayer or just saying farewell. The knocking occurs mostly at night, and it invariably wakes me up. When I hear it my first reaction is to wait for some more noise or to try to find the source of it since it sounds external and as near as my headboard or my window. Once

I realize the kind of noise it is, I just sit up and say some spontaneous prayers, and then go back to sleep, blessing "whoever was calling."

Some ten years ago we learned that an elderly lady, the mother of a friend of ours, was gravely ill in the hospital. When early one morning I heard the familiar three knocks, I sat up, waited a moment and then asked my husband if he had heard the knocking. He said he had not. Intuitively I said: "Then, Mrs. F. is dying." We looked at the clock on the radio and it showed 2:10 a.m. I said prayers for her soul, wishing her a peaceful transition and a loving welcome. The next day we were informed that the lady had died and were told about the funeral arrangements. Two days later we visited our friend and his family to offer our condolences and talked a while about her and her passing. Our friend commented on the peaceful way in which she had died, and added that it had been much more peaceful than his father's death, less than a year earlier. Then he said his mother had passed away at 2:10 a.m. My husband and I told him about my experience two nights earlier at exactly the hour of her death.

**Chapter 31**

# A Mother's Love

Paramahansa Yogananda once said that a mother's love is the purest example of God's love on earth. I certainly had a taste of it during my mother's life, for she had a gentle way of dispensing it to her children as needed, without fanfare.

I lived at my parents' home until I got married, at age twenty-five, and a year later left my country with my husband, not to return for the next five years. There was nothing I missed more in the world during those first years than my mother's reassuring presence. I shed a lot of quiet tears at the beginning, feeling homesick and expecting a baby in a foreign land that didn't seem safe to me, without the benefit of her love and wise experience. With two political assassinations and the Vietnam War raging at that time, 1968 was not a very good year to come to the United States. Only my husband's patience and understanding and the love I had for him made my first years in the United States more bearable.

After my father's death in 1965, my mother was left with three children under the age of fifteen (plus five older ones) and very little income. I never saw her despair or complain. By God's grace and the modest salaries of two of my brothers and myself, we didn't have to go through any economical crises, and by any logic I don't know why we didn't.

One thing I never saw my parents do was worry about money, and I assure you we were not rich, by any stretch of the imagination. What I saw in them was a great confidence in always having enough material means to take care of their large family. I can say that I have honored that trait well myself. With just one income (my husband's salary as a teacher), we too have managed to live well for a low middle-income family of four. In our home I take care of money matters, since my husband never showed much interest in managing it. Whenever he asks if we have any money, I am very fond of answering him that we have enough and more than enough, because that is the way I see it at all times. And it is so. It might be just my mind, but I have seen it work for a long time.

My mother, Aura Rosa de Moreno, lived for many years in her home in Bogotá with one of my sisters, who had also become a widow, with two daughters. Although later Myriam remarried and moved away, she always kept close contact with our mother. But fate dealt another hard blow to my sister's life when her second husband was kidnapped and murdered in early 1990. (Her first husband, a lawyer, had died in an automobile accident). In the face of her new tragedy, my sister left the country in pain and rage and headed for Italy with her baby, then four years old. My mother kept the two older girls who were already close to finishing high school. A group of Catholic nuns running a hospice for the elderly in Rome, welcomed Myriam and her child in their quarters and gave her a job and much needed moral support.

In 1993, at age seventy-nine, my mother's health was not bad, except for signs of a slight loss of memory. With her two granddaughters half way through college and one of them married, she decided to sell her house and do some traveling overseas, mostly to visit my sister in Italy and me in the United States. In the summer of 1994 she left Colombia with one of her granddaughters for a short visit to Russia and then on to Rome. At her age we didn't want her to travel alone, so by the end of the summer I went to Colombia to pick her up after her return from Europe, and bring her with me to the United States.

It was my turn to care for my mother, and I welcomed the privilege of doing it. I had to confess that the idea was hers, and I was grateful she thought of it, because we tend to think or hope that our parents will live forever, and they don't. Nine months, like the time I lived in her womb, was all I was allowed to have her for myself.

Long talks, short walks, a little gardening, a loving Chihuahua to take a nap with, a hug and a kiss and a game of cards were most of the simple pleasures she enjoyed. But going to downtown San Antonio, to the River Walk, and taking a ride on a barge, was tops with her. About once a month we would take the bus and go somewhere together: a church, a restaurant, a mall, or even a parade. Like me, she liked shopping and the outdoors.

A strange thing happened to us one day when we were downtown. After a fair amount of walking around doing a little shopping, my mother and I went to a restaurant to have lunch. There I noticed my coin purse was missing; inside were my student bus card (for the use of public buses at half-price) and my mother's senior citizen's ID for the same purpose, plus about six dollars in change and small bills. I remembered having used the little purse downtown that afternoon, to put some change in. It wasn't a big problem, since I had enough money with me to pay for lunch and buses; just the inconvenience of having to do more paperwork and take the time to go get new ID cards. After lunch we headed back home, a good forty-minute bus ride.

About ten minutes into the ride, a tall black woman I had never seen got on the bus, looked at us and said: "You lost some IDs today, didn't you? I have them, and I want to return them to you." "All the money is there, too," she added, holding my little orange and black cloth purse. I asked her how she knew it was ours; she answered: "By your mother's photo," and handed me the purse. Delighted to have our IDs, I thanked her twice and said to her, "You are an angel." She moved on to take a seat two rows back on the opposite side of us. Two stops down the road, she got off the bus.

That shook me up a little more. Why would that woman get on the same bus hours later, far from the place where I had lost my purse, and from the stop where my mother and I had caught the bus, just to return our IDs, and then get off so soon? It made no sense to me. My mother's picture wasn't even a clear one, and the woman had not held the picture in front of us to compare features, nor had she taken the time to study my mother's face. (My student bus card did not have a photo on it). Was the woman really an angel? I smiled and thanked God again.

Another delightful little "coincidence" happened to us one day after an outing. We were about seven blocks from home, but didn't want to cross a wide busy street, and, besides, my mother was tired. So I told her I was going to call Cliff to come pick us up. As I was getting my coin ready to make the call, my mother asked, "How much is it for a telephone call?" "Twenty-five cents," I answered. Her comment was, "Ah, that's expensive, isn't it?" (The reason she thought it was expensive was that calls from public phones in Colombia cost only the equivalent of two American cents.) I understood what she meant and told her, "Yes, it is a little expensive, but God sometimes returns my coin." (He does.)

I put my coin in the slot, the phone swallowed it as usual, I made my call to Cliff and then hung up. The moment the receiver was back on its hook, my coin fell by itself into the coin return receptacle at the bottom. That surprised my mother quite a bit. To me it was just funny, to see how God didn't want to make a liar out of me at that moment.

Having a coin returned to me was nothing new; it has been happening for years, but only when there is a real need of any kind, never by capricious will or just because I want to prove a point. When the incident in front of my mother occurred, it had not crossed my mind that my coin would be returned like that. As a college student in the eighties and early nineties, I used to call the house quite often from school, to check on my two teenage boys, to make sure that everyone, including the dogs, had been fed, to remind them of their chores, or to inform my husband of any change in my evening class schedule that would affect the time he would have to pick me up at the 'park and ride,' etc. Sometimes making the call meant not having the exact change left for bus fare, or having to walk to the cafeteria or a vending machine to buy a snack I didn't need in order to change a bill. Being short of breath most of the time, any excess walking makes my chest even tighter, which then forces me to pause and rest a few minutes if I want to avoid having an asthma attack. These are the kinds of situations in which a higher power has been at work in small but relevant ways, such as returning my quarter without me asking, but oh, so timely. On a few occasions I have been mentally instructed to look into the telephone's coin return for the coin I need. Once I even heard the coin drop as my inner voice was speaking. I am not in the habit of searching for coins in telephone booths or fond of obtaining a service by cheating, but these little coincidences have made things a little easier for me at times.

When it occurred to me that I might be the cause of these phenomena, through the power of thought, I tried (more than once) to test myself by concentrating on the action of a coin falling into the receptacle, without any luck. Well, nothing left to do but to smile and be grateful. After all the wonderful things I've seen, why question little miracles? Will I ever learn that when we get our stubborn will and pride out of the way, Divine Mind does show us that we don't have to struggle all the time? I trust I will.

The Divine Plan was at work again when we applied for an extension on my mother's original six-month visa. We wanted her to stay with us one more year, but Immigration extended it for six more months, only. Because traveling with her to Colombia by the end of the additional six months would mean missing or interrupting my fall semester at school, we decided to take my mother back to Colombia as soon as my spring semester ended in mid-May and, taking advantage of my husband's annual leave scheduled for that same period, have a short vacation with him in Barranquilla. (Cliff had not been to Colombia in seventeen years.) Another thing that worried us a little was that my mother had gotten a swelling in one arm. We had taken her to the doctor twice in the two months since we had noticed it (he diagnosed it as swollen lymph glands), without seeing much improvement. I wanted her to have some good unconventional acupuncture and herbal treatments as soon as we got to Colombia.

With four sons living in Barranquilla, my mother would have to take her pick which son to stay with first. Being the considerate person she had always been, my mother talked of helping to pay for her keeping, something my brothers, or Cliff and I, would not even think about, unless big medical expenses would be necessary, which at her age was always possible.

We arrived in Barranquilla in mid-May 1994, the day before Mother's Day (same date as in the United States). One sister living in the interior of Colombia had flown in with two of her children to welcome her back, too. The celebration the next day was memorable. Six of my mother's eight children and most of her grandchildren got together for a family reunion like I had not seen in ages. No less than twenty-five members of the family were there to honor our mother/grandmother. Only my sister Myriam and my brother Milton (living in Italy and Costa Rica) were absent.

On Monday I tried to make an appointment with an acupuncturist, but my sister Stella (married to a pharmacist) thought she should consult first with her brother-in-law, a doctor living in another town. When he heard about my mother's symptoms, he advised us to take her immediately to see an oncologist. We shuddered at the recommendation but hurried to make an emergency appointment for that same day. Upon examining and X-raying my mother, the doctor (a woman) called my sister and me apart and told us my mother had an advanced case of breast cancer, already spreading to her lungs, and showed us the X-rays.

It was plain to see. The cancer had probably been there for years already.

Fear, confusion and guilt gripped us both, at once. The doctor didn't think the cancer was operable at this point but, nevertheless, she recommended that we see another oncologist, a surgeon, and gave us the name of one. When we saw him, he convinced us that a biopsy was needed, and performed one by the end of that same week. It confirmed the bad news. We regretted having put my mother through it, afterwards, since she now had a very painful spot, and all for nothing.

In view of the gravity of my mother's condition, we immediately contacted our brother and sister overseas. One of the contacts had to be made by letter since we didn't have my brother's telephone number in Costa Rica. As I was writing his letter, I remembered that about three weeks before leaving San Antonio, my mother had told me one morning about "a very strange, short dream" she had just had. I now was seeing a new significance to it. This is what she had said that morning:

"*Alonso* (my father) *came and took me flying to a beautiful place, but not of this earth.*" End of the dream.

Then she added, "What do you think it means?" Being myself used to traveling in my dreams to other worlds, including seeing my father at least twice (once, from a bridge, in a garden-like setting, and another time while he was in a state of meditation in some kind of lighted cave (in life he had not been a meditator or even a prayerful person as far as I could remember), I told her it probably meant that he was living in that beautiful place and had wanted to show it to her. In the light of the present events, I saw it as a premonition of her death.

Once we learned my sister Myriam would be coming from Italy to be at our mother's side, we knew she would be in the best of hands, since Myriam had by then been caring for elderly patients for several years. Stella would have to go back home to manage one of the two pharmacies her husband owned, and I had some things to take care of in San Antonio.

Cliff and I returned to the States. I had planned to take a summer class at the university and needed to cancel it and get a refund on my tuition. I also needed to organize bills, paperwork and household chores for Cliff and the boys to take care of in my absence. Myriam kept me informed by telephone on my mother's condition, which was deteriorating rapidly. We agreed I should return to Colombia as soon as possible.

Within three days of getting my letter, my brother Milton left Costa Rica for Colombia, without worrying much about not collecting several weeks' salary as a racehorse trainer. He had not seen our mother in almost ten years.

My mother didn't complain much about pain during her illness, and for that we prayed and were very grateful to God. The biopsy incision on her neck, however, was somewhat painful all along and proved more detrimental than helpful, since from that moment on we saw her condition decline very fast. She lived only thirty seven days from the date of her diagnosis, being confined to bed and under oxygen only the last three days of her life, which was remarkable.

If it had been up to her doctor, however, my mother would have been subjected to a less dignified and peaceful end. On the 19th of June (Monday evening) he came to examine her, and then sat with me at the dining table to make recommendations. He said it was going to be a long while for my mother yet, and advised us to put her in a hospital for more testing and more aggressive treatment. I absolutely refused to do any such thing, in her hopeless condition, and told the "buzzard," no! My brothers and my sister Myriam all agreed. The doctor was not amused and even had some threatening words for us. All the while my mother had heard our heated conversation.

Our most immediate concern was to get another tank of oxygen for my mother since the first one was getting low. Being late when we noticed the tank was almost empty, we were unsuccessful in finding a place open, and decided to wait until Tuesday morning to order a new one, praying the tank in use would last the night.

My mother died that same night at 4:30 in the morning. My sister, a niece and myself were sleeping in the same room. We had checked her at around mid- night and changed her (since she was receiving fluids intravenously), and then we had gone to sleep. Myriam woke me up around 4:30 to help her with another changing, and we even had my mother help a little bit, lifting herself a tad. As soon as she was changed, as we were fixing her covers, she gave her last breath, peacefully, without a sound. Within a couple of minutes everyone in the house was around her bed weeping. One of my brothers took the oxygen cannula away from her, but decided to leave the oxygen open for the tank to empty. It lasted no more than two extra minutes. Was that a coincidence? I don't think so. We knew right then that it all had happened on purpose, very much in keeping with her wise, considerate nature. She had just elected to go gently, without causing any fuss. (Exactly one year earlier, June 20th 1994, my husband's father had passed away in Pensacola, Florida.)

In another part of town, just about the time of her passing, my mother was visiting one of her favorite granddaughters, in spirit. My niece saw her clearly, sitting at the end of her bed, and without a second thought said, "Grandma, you're well!" As my niece sat up, two things happened – the apparition vanished and the telephone rang. It was one of us in the house calling to inform my brother Humberto and his family about my mother's passing.

Three days after my mother's funeral I returned to San Antonio. My sister Myriam went back to Rome two months later, and my brother Milton decided to stay in Colombia longer to explore the possibilities of a business venture. He later opened a restaurant in partnership with another brother, but met with failure within a year.

A mother's love transcends earthly life such as few other loves ever will. After my mother's passing in June 1995, she has found ways to let her children know that she still cares by means of dreams and little miracles, all of which have served to comfort us.

In August 1996 my husband and I went to Costa Rica, without much planning ahead (a week at the most) just wanting to look the place over for retirement possibilities within the next few years. We stayed in the capital, San José, and made short one-day trips to nearby towns, to get away from the busy rhythm of San José. (Any corner of the country can be reached from the capital, within a two-to-four hour drive). On the fourth day of our stay, I suggested that we visit a national rainforest park for the day. Cliff was reluctant to go just then and suggested another place, but my determination won. We took a bus to the town nearest the park, and there contracted a taxi to take us to the entrance of the park and pick us up three hours later. It was a misty and rainy day in the park's mountainous terrain, but we were well prepared for that eventuality. Very few people were touring the site that day; we only encountered and greeted a small group of Italians there. Even the forest animals were quiet, with only a sporadic birdcall interrupting the hushed mood of nature. We had a most tranquil walk down to a river at the bottom of the park and then up to the entrance to wait for our taxi.

Since a direct bus to San José was not scheduled to leave that afternoon from the small town we were at, we took one to Cartago, where we would find buses leaving for the capital every half-hour. It was around four in the afternoon when we arrived in Cartago, and we were feeling a bit hungry. After walking around a few blocks and not finding anything more appealing, we decided to go to Pizza Hut; their food was nothing to brag about, but it was filling.

Once we ate we headed towards the bus station, some three blocks away. As we were nearing a street crossing, from the opposite direction my brother Milton was walking towards us, as surprised to see us, as we were to see him. What an amazing thing and a beautiful encounter for us. He had arrived in Costa Rica six days earlier, without either of us knowing about each other's plans. Cliff had not seen my brother in twenty-seven years. My brother recognized me first and then figured out that the "gringo" walking with me must be Cliff. As we sat on a bench in a nearby park, it occurred to all of us that my mother must have had something to do with this delightful surprise. If not for the few days I had seen Milton in Colombia a year earlier when our mother died, it would have been very hard to recognize each other, because without that short reacquaintance, it would have been twenty-seven years for me, too, without seeing my brother. My brother spent the next two days (our last in Costa Rica) with us, talking about all the things we hadn't had a chance to talk about while my mother was dying, since at that time he had stayed in a different house and we had had too much on our minds to just sit down and chat. We were very grateful for this heaven sent opportunity.

Very recently my brother Victor told me over the telephone about an uncanny experience he and some relatives and friends had in church, in Barranquilla on June 20, 1997, when they attended a mass on the second anniversary of my mother's death. As the mass ended, several people on both sides of the isle saw my mother walking down the center isle towards the front door. Their jaws just dropped in amazement. They followed the "apparition" to discover, outside the church, that the woman was an elderly lady they didn't know, with no resemblance whatsoever to my mother; probably a habitual churchgoer. Those who experienced the occurrence (more than half a dozen adults and some children), however, had no doubt in their minds they had seen my mother.

# Chapter 32

# Personal Reflections

If you asked me what I think of my life, I would have to say, half jokingly, "Straaange!" and then I would have to ask God, half seriously also: "Is all this pain really necessary?"

Living is a pain in varying degrees for every human being. It is so because we are truly Spirit learning to live in the flesh, in matter. We all need to master the art of living, but it is not an easy endeavor. We bring with us to this earth tasks and goals to fulfill, along with the powers of wisdom, will and choice to help us work it out. The trouble is, early on we become forgetful and let preoccupation with the externals throw us off balance. By middle age or so we realize we have been practically "sleeping on the job" and, if our spiritual nature is awakening then, try to make up for lost time and find out in a hurry what our "mission" in life might be. We might never remember exactly what the mission is, but there are "divine hints" being dropped all along for us to notice. We all lose some precious time in our youth, and the pitiful thing is that we know better, but there is no use crying over spilt milk. The truth is, there is rejoicing in heaven any time a prodigal son or daughter finds the way home. So why be discouraged when we take a few temporary (and sometimes necessary) detours? Sooner or later we all will make it home in great style.

Illness has hindered my physical being considerably for almost thirty years, but it has taught me precious lessons in courage, compassion and trust, among other things. As for learning patience, I can't make any claims yet. Anger and frustration also creep in now and then (my husband and children can tell you that), but those feelings don't last long; there is always something good to replace them with. The truth is I love life and everything about it and feel grateful to be around, and if I can be of use to someone, lovelier still.

I have been asked a few times if the NDEs have changed my life a great deal. They have, but not drastically. Spiritual matters, for example, have interested me from the beginning. I remember as a child, in my hometown's church, wanting so much to touch all the sacred symbols decorating the altar, as well as the plates and the chalices on it, but being told that girls and women were not allowed near it. "It's not just," I thought, "it makes no sense." More than once I sneaked in and touched at least the linens of the altar, to my great satisfaction and no punishment from heaven. That all changed after the Ecumenical Council in 1963, when women were allowed more participation in the rites of the Catholic Church, but by then I had already left the Church and had discovered some of the spiritual treasures of Hinduism.

A dissatisfaction with organized religion, but at the same time an intense desire for spiritual growth, has been associated with the NDE, and I fill that profile well, except that in my case those feelings were present as early as fifteen years of age, many years before my first NDE. As to going to church, I do attend a few, (mostly metaphysical ), when the spirit moves me, if the music is good, or if they are offering a class or lecture I want to attend, but at this point I don't want to belong to any church. Church and religion have their place and can do a lot of good for many, but as for me, I haven't found yet a more sacred, quiet and comfortable church to worship at, than my own heart. There is no replacement for the intimate joy and sweetness of direct communion with God in your own heart; for these moments with the divine more than anything else, I strive.

A thirst for knowledge after the near-death experience is another characteristic more or less common among experiencers. It is true I started college after my first NDE (in my early forties) but I would have done so regardless, since I had plans for my studies all along. I was simply waiting for my children to grow up enough and for my health troubles to subside. God has given me a good mind, and I thoroughly enjoyed my studies, without letting illness (which is a daily struggle) keep me away from the pleasure of learning. Teachers and classmates alike on several occasions expressed their admiration for my tenacity, willingness and quality of work in spite of my sometimes slightly disruptive coughing and puffing in class.

I think every human being has traits of potential virtues, and talents worth developing. It is our duty to do so and to encourage others to test their wings, too. Going back to school I accomplished more than getting a bachelor's and a master's degree; it was also an opportunity to "teach without a classroom" about spiritual matters, not by pushing any particular belief, but by touching others' hearts gently, making them aware of their own goodness and the Source of all goodness. What sweet soul nurturing there was in those one-to-one or small group spiritual exchanges. The important thing is that in doing our life's work, whatever it is, we honor Spirit (God) in ourselves and all. Love is the most desirable virtue, we hear, but I think good will towards all (the Golden Rule) will suffice, because it is love in action.

IANDS (International Association for Near-Death Studies) has done an excellent job in sharing information and sponsoring study groups all over the United States, where experiencers, supporters and interested people can meet regularly to share, learn and discuss the subject of the near-death experience and related phenomena. I have belonged to such a group in San Antonio since 1992 and highly recommend it to anyone who wants to learn more about this fascinating matter. One of the wonderful things a support group like IANDS does for those experiencers who might need help, is to dispel to a great extend the sense of confusion, dissatisfaction and even anger some of them feel after returning to life in the body. Within the group they find a safe and understanding environment in which to reveal and discuss their experiences, without pressure or judgment.

I would like to close this chapter with a Russian saying I learned as a young woman: "Life is good and living is good." I am grateful for mine.

## ABOUT THE AUTHOR

GLORIA M. GIESEKE was born in Colombia, South America in 1941 and has lived on every continent in the past 30 years. She has been a student of foreign languages and world religions and holds a Master of Arts degree in Spanish literature from the University of Texas at San Antonio. She is currently preparing a Spanish version of her first book, "Where is the Music?: The Multiple Near-Death Experiences of a World Traveler." A member of IANDS (International Association for Near-death Studies), Mrs. Gieseke resides with her husband and the younger of their two sons in San Antonio, Texas.

# Order Form

Name

Address

City                  State        Zip

Phone               e-mail

Please send me _____ copies of "Where is the Music?" for $14.95 each plus $3.00 each for shipping and handling. Texas residents please add 7.75% sales tax.

Mail this form, plus your check or money order to:

Password Publications
8611 Cape Valley
San Antonio, TX 78227

**Comments are appreciated.**
Tel 675-7592
E-mail: gloriagie@yahoo.com
cliffgie@hotmail.com
cliffgie@swbell.com

# Order Form

Name _____

Address _____

City _____ State _____ Zip _____

Phone _____ e-mail _____

Please send me _____ copies of "Where is the Music?"
for $14.95 each plus $3.00 each for shipping and handling.
Texas residents please add 7.75% sales tax.

Mail this form, plus your check or money order to:

Password Publications
8611 Cape Valley
San Antonio, TX 78227

**Comments are appreciated.**
**Tel 675-7592**
**E-mail: gloriagie@yahoo.com**
**cliffgie@hotmail.com**
cliffgie@swbell.com